Penguin Education

Penguin Education Specials
General Editor: Willem van der Eyken

The Politics of Education
Edward Boyle and Anthony Crosland
in conversation with Maurice Kogan

Maurice Kogan is Professor of Government and Social
Administration at Brunel University. He was previously an
administrator in the Department of Education and Science,
where he was Edward Boyle's Private Secretary for nearly
three years. He was secretary to the Plowden Committee
on primary education. He left the DES to start the Brunel
University Hospital Organization Research Unit and is now
particularly concerned with studies of the organization and
administration of the social services.

The Politics of Education

Edward Boyle and Anthony Crosland
in conversation with Maurice Kogan

Penguin Education

Penguin Education
Penguin Books Ltd
Harmondsworth, Middlesex, England
Penguin Books Inc., 7110 Ambassador Road,
Baltimore, Md 21207, USA
Penguin Books Australia Ltd,
Ringwood, Victoria, Australia
Penguin Books Canada Ltd,
41 Steelcase Road West, Markham,
Ontario, Canada
Penguin Books (N.Z.) Ltd,
182–190 Wairau Road, Auckland 10, New Zealand

First published 1971
Reprinted 1974
Copyright © Edward Boyle, Anthony Crosland
and Maurice Kogan, 1971
Introduction copyright © Maurice Kogan, 1971

Made and printed in Great Britain by
C. Nicholls & Company Ltd,
The Philips Park Press, Manchester
Set in Intertype Times

Contents

Preface 7

Introduction by Maurice Kogan 11
The Political Impetus 12
Politics and Risk Taking 13
The Ideological Frame of Reference 16
The Changing Role of the Department 25
The Minister as Manager 31
Ministers and the Machinery of Government 34
The Minister and his Department 39
Ministers and Pressure Groups 44
The Impact of the Politician on Policies 48
Notes 60

Edward Boyle 65
The Attraction of Politics 69
Becoming a Cabinet Minister 72
On Being a Minister 81
The Constraints on the Minister's Power:
His Freedom of Action 102
What Can a Secretary of State Achieve? 137

Anthony Crosland 145
The Attraction of Politics 149
Becoming a Cabinet Minister 152
On Being a Minister 156
The Constraints on the Minister's Power:
His Freedom of Action 159
What Can a Secretary of State Achieve? 187

Index 201

Preface

In this book two of the ablest politicians to emerge since the 1939–45 war discuss their role as Minister and Secretary of State for Education. The conversations took place in the autumn and early winter of 1970 – immediately after the General Election had taken Anthony Crosland out of office as Secretary of State for Local Government and Regional Planning and Edward Boyle had resigned from politics to become Vice-Chancellor of the University of Leeds.

The author is grateful to the two former Ministers for the open and patient way in which they answered and helped clarify his questions. Willem van der Eyken's contribution went well beyond skilful editing to directly helping to develop the main ideas as they emerged in the text.

Much of the information and some of the arguments in the introduction and prefatory notes were assembled by Graham Macklin. The author is also grateful to Elna Andersson, Josephine Brown, Ulla Kogan and Sally Marshall for the typing of successive drafts.

Essential notes are given at the foot of the page. The numbered notes in the text refer to further notes on pages 60–63.

Organization of Department of Education and Science during
Anthony Crosland's period of office (January 1965 to August 1967)

Secretary of State

2 Ministers of State (Higher Education
and Science; Schools)

2 Parliamentary Under-Secretaries of
State (Arts and Sport†)

| Legal Adviser | Senior Chief Inspector | Directors of the Science and Victoria and Albert Museums | Secretary and Chief Inspector for Wales |

10 Under-Secretaries

*The official ranks given here are generic civil service grades.
When the political chief is a Minister, the officials are as
named here. When he is a Secretary of State they are called
Permanent Under-Secretary of State, Deputy Under-Secretary
of State, Assistant Under-Secretary of State, Assistant Secretary,
Principal

†Jennie Lee was made a Minister of State in 1967

‡Architects and Building is under an Assistant Secretary who
used to refer directly to a Deputy Secretary

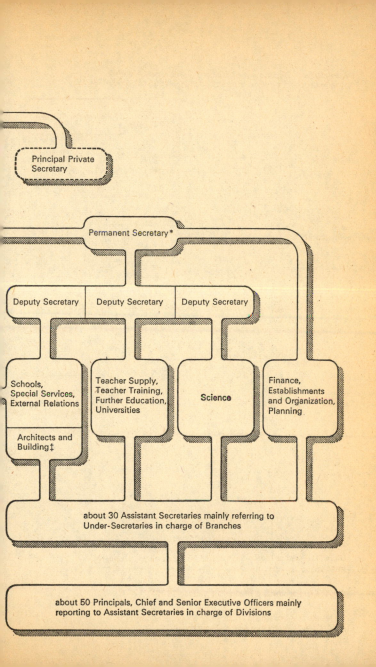

Principal Private
Secretary

Permanent Secretary*

Deputy Secretary

Deputy Secretary

Deputy Secretary

Schools,
Special Services,
External Relations

Teacher Supply,
Teacher Training,
Further Education,
Universities

Science

Finance,
Establishments
and Organization,
Planning

Architects and
Building‡

about 30 Assistant Secretaries mainly referring to
Under-Secretaries in charge of Branches

about 50 Principals, Chief and Senior Executive Officers mainly
reporting to Assistant Secretaries in charge of Divisions

Introduction

Maurice Kogan

In the pages that follow, Edward Boyle and Anthony Crosland answer questions put to them on their role as Ministers of Education – the service that they led between them for five of its most formative years. The questions were prepared in advance and the answers were spontaneously given. They have since been modified, but not much. There has been rather more modification of the questions put to them whenever the strength of the answer revealed the inadequacy of the question. Neither Minister saw each other's script before proof stage, though many of the questions put to Edward Boyle were improved after the two days of conversation with Anthony Crosland. Both Ministers saw, but take no responsibility for, this introduction. Indeed on some points both disagree with my interpretation. But the statement of differences in perception between two Ministers, and between them and a former administrator in their Ministry, was thought to be a valuable part of the book.

The book is intended to analyse the role of the Minister rather than to discuss the main policies which they promoted. It is even less intended to portray individual personality except when this might account for the differences in the way in which they played their roles. Policies and personality do, of course, break through; the dialogues show how individual are the two men's styles of expression and their approach to the main issues of politics and organization.

In considering their roles Edward Boyle and Anthony Crosland answer such questions as: What draws able men to the chancy and sometimes messy career of the politician? How do they differ in attitudes and function from their senior civil servants? Who makes educational policy? How does a Minister of Education relate to the Prime Minister, Cabinet, the Treasury and the rest of the Whitehall machine? Do MPs have a say in policy making? What are the relationships between

central and local government and the more informal power
networks of teacher and local authority associations, the press,
the academic intelligentsia? What impact do the statutory
advisory councils have? And what can a Minister *do* – what
constraints are there on his actions?

The Political Impetus

Superficially, Crosland and Boyle share many personal charac-
teristics. Both are of those Oxford generations, of the 1930s
and 1940s, which produced so many of our political leaders
and which, it could be argued, provide the accents, if not the
vocabulary, of much of our present political discourse.* Both
have 'something' about religion in their backgrounds – Crosland's family were Plymouth Brethren and Boyle was for
long thought to be high Anglican; both are now probably
agnostic, and pragmatic about life in general and politics in
particular. Crosland has considerable training and analytical
strength in economics, and Boyle no training but an enduring
interest.

Crosland and Boyle are attractive and stimulating men –
good to listen to and to be with.† Yet, though they attract a
large number of friends, there is much of the self-critical and
even of the isolate in them. We must not psychologize, as
Crosland implies at the beginning of his interview – but is
there something about politics which attracts those who want
to go it to the top alone? Unlike some Ministers, however, the
unavoidable isolation of being the top man in a large Department did not cause them to betray their values as intellectuals
– they expected to be argued with and to take as well as they
gave, from subordinates as well as friends.

Both were early committed to the political life. Crosland

*This crop of Oxonians included Edward Heath, Harold Wilson, Roy
Jenkins, Reginald Maudling, Richard Crossman, Michael Stewart, Denis
Healey, Anthony Wedgwood Benn and Patrick Gordon Walker.

†Anthony Crosland must have a considerable hold over the general public. An Opinion Research Centre survey showed that 24 per cent of those
asked 'Do you know which of these are Ministers in the Government?'
named Crosland (*Sunday Times*, 4 April 1971). He had left office ten months
before. In comparison, 30 per cent named Roy Jenkins, but also only 13 per
cent named John Davies.

turned away from the career as a don or a writer that could have easily been his; he is a writer of lucid prose that carries new ideas to the forefront of political debate. Boyle was, paradoxically (because of the 'insider' position which he is at some pains to refute), more limited in his choices. He was soon seen as a remarkable man of his generation. Churchill made him a junior Minister at the age of twenty-nine. Both he and Crosland were early seen as front-runners.

Both men chose politics because they wanted to have an impact on affairs. Both are clear that this is the arena in which major decisions and fragments of history are made, and they wanted to be in them. Both admit only grudgingly the tenuousness of a Minister's hold over the decision-making process, and this is a point which will be examined, from an equally biased administrator's point of view, later in this introduction.

Their life-styles reflect their general philosophies. Boyle came from a relatively wealthy family, with a house in the country and in London, while Crosland's father was an administrative civil servant. Both now live unlavishly but well. Boyle is ensconced in the Vice-Chancellor's Lodge at Leeds University surrounded by new colleagues, his books and about twenty yards of gramophone records in chronological order running along the side of a studio. Crosland, too, lives with the elegance of taste rather than affluence. What he has, he and his wife have earned. So in their pattern of living and in their public statements both politicians have proclaimed the virtues of the good secular life, of rationality, tolerance, of a good visual and general environment, and high consumption for all. This expansionist, tolerant and utilitarian attitude fitted them well for the ethos of the 1960s – the era which they helped to shape and govern.

Yet, as we shall see later on, the differences in attitudes, objectives and achievements are more marked than their surface similarities lead us to think.

Politics and Risk Taking

Politicians are risk takers. Crosland rather than Boyle demonstrates the risks of the political life though Boyle, too, lost office in 1964 after being a Minister for ten years. Boyle's work in remoulding the educational attitudes of the Conservative Party had begun to crumble under the suspicion engendered by his stand on race relations and the abolition of the death penalty, also under the force of the reaction against progressive methods and the integrative organization of education which was epitomized by the two Black Papers.[1]

We expect our politicians to be many things – our communal prophets and oracles, the risk takers who at one moment may have the eyes of millions on them and possess the rewards of office, but the next moment may be back (if re-elected) on £3250 a year – less than the maximum salary of a Principal in the civil service – without an official car, without Ministerial salary, without briefing, without the whole apparatus of official publicity and with reduced chances of returning to Ministerial office, for there are always alternative Ministers waiting to take their place.*

So Crosland, who is now fifty-two years old, might well have to wait until he is fifty-six or fifty-seven, or sixty-two or sixty-three, before a chance of office comes again. He is explicit about the extent to which he, in common with other politicians, selected a life of insecurity:

Unlike the civil servant, he [the politician] is constantly going to be attacked in Parliament, criticized in the press, heckled at public meetings, badgered by endless and often hostile deputations.... He will spend some time finding a seat in the first place, nursing it, and getting elected. Then he's liable to lose his seat, as I did in 1955, and has got to find another one and get elected again. If he becomes a Minister he will suddenly lose his job because his party is chucked out of office at a General Election.... If I look back on my life, insecurity has been a very marked characteristic (see p. 151).

What does not emerge clearly from the dialogues is that it is not only a risky but also a dog's life – an artificial existence spent less in the comforts of an exclusive club than in the com-

*The difference in the availability of this facility – controlled exposure through official press releases, Ministerial speeches on set occasions, forewords to Departmental reports, Parliamentary occasions – is very marked. Michael Foot made this point well on the day Harold Wilson came into power in 1964 – that even though a majority of six in the Commons made for a precarious government, all the advantages of control over the machine had now swung in Labour's favour ('Election Special', BBC-1).

pany of egocentrics where the country's most ambitious talkers are compelled to listen far more than they may talk. The all-night sitting, the tedium of constituency work, the evenings in the company of the faithful – if they choose to be faithful – are essential to it. Yet these aspects of his life place a burden on the energies and affect the perspective of the politician who must also, as Minister, try to be the effective and reliable visionary. It is this process that makes the intellectual in politics a rarity. The politician has to deal with the ruthless and the uncouth as well as the spontaneous and the idealistic. The civil servant is protected from this.

While the young administrative civil servant begins to take his own decisions within two years of leaving university, and contributes to policy quite early on, or acts as a private secretary with a ringside seat on Ministerial and Parliamentary activities – all at a certain and ever increasing pensionable salary – the potential young Crosland or Boyle has to work to reach a marginally safe seat perhaps one or two General Elections hence. If he is fortunate and becomes an MP he is consulted, as a back-bencher, on policies in general terms, when and if Ministers think fit.* If exceptionally lucky he might become a junior Minister in his early forties, by which time a civil servant of Crosland's or Boyle's ability will be an Assistant Secretary or an Under-Secretary who has been acquiring expertise, confidence and a say in affairs of state, day in and day out, for the previous twenty years.†

And even when in office, as Boyle puts it in talking of his chances of getting one of the top Ministerial positions, 'You can get so far in politics by enthusiasm and, if you like, by ability; above that it's very much a matter of your position in the party, your relationship to the total picture, your image at a given time, as well as your leader's views about the composition he requires' (see p. 70). The risks must make politicians sensitive to public opinion in a way that neither the

*See p. 165 for Anthony Crosland's view of the MP's role and pp. 119-21 for Edward Boyle's.

†The few MPs who reach office have four or five years as junior Ministers, and of these only a small number become full Ministers with perhaps another two to four years in office. See J. Blondel, *Voters, Parties and Leaders*, Penguin, 1963, pp. 156–7.

virtually permanently established Ministers in some other countries, nor leading politicians in local authorities, need be (Sweden, where the social democrats have held office since 1932, Durham and the pre-1964 LCC are examples). And whether they accept it or not, they are bound to take the middle or short-term view. In the long run, they are all out of office.

It is, perhaps, this unpredictability rather than the severity of the penalties which must hurt most. S. E. Finer, in a survey of Ministerial resignations from 1855 to 1965, concluded that instead of the survival of a Minister depending on the severity of the error or the extent of Parliamentary criticism 'it is the haphazard consequence of a fortuitous concomitance of personal, party and political temper'.[2] Politicians seem to move like the existential victims of circumstance in a post-war Cocteau film. The sense of *les jeux sont faits* to some extent explains the failure of Ministers to think in terms not so much of objectives – both Crosland and Boyle were unusual in doing this – as of their long-range programming and detailed articulation.

The contrast between the insecurity and slowness of achievement, and the prizes given when office is gained, inevitably marks the work of the politician. Neither Boyle nor Crosland agrees that insecurity affects their sense of priorities or causes them to temper principles by considerations of political feasibility. Both more readily give witness to the extent to which random success with the Prime Minister, with their colleagues, with that Old Testament god, the Treasury, and with the press, affect their success as Ministers.

The Ideological Frame of Reference

Boyle and Crosland's personal and political beliefs fitted and contributed to the complex movements of ideas affecting the education service in the 1960s. Their particular style and contribution were, however, individual.

Boyle's ideology is less easy than Crosland's to epitomize if only because radical conservatism is inherently eclectic and uncertain about which values to preserve and which to test hard or reject. He was idiosyncratic, moreover, among Conservative Ministers in his deep commitment to the educational service: 'After the Treasury, there is no Department in which I should more like the chance of serving than the Ministry of Education' he said on joining it after the Suez crisis.

Yet his commitment to education, like that of, say, Lord Eccles and Richard Hornby, raises questions for the historians of political ideology. How can we differentiate Boyle from Crosland or, say, Shirley Williams? For on some issues Boyle displays an etatist radicalism which implies more a belief in communal action than in Selsdon man doing it alone, and he sides with many Labour politicians on such issues as the abolition of the death penalty, or race relations.* In Crosland there is not only radicalism but also a strong belief in rational and pragmatically justifiable action – the claim of intellectual Tories from Burke to Angus Maude and not at all in the evangelical mode of Lansbury or Bevan. These are, perhaps, preferences of style and strategy as well as of principles and policy. Crosland's books argue for a major shift in economic, social and political power, through more subtle and, he would claim, appropriate mechanisms than the traditional Labour politics of nationalization (see pp. 19 and 60, n.10). He claims to belong to the populist tradition of, say, Keir Hardie.†

Boyle is heir to no particular party tradition. His philosophy tells us nothing about the general trend of post-war conservatism, as Mrs Thatcher's decisions and declared policies since his time have since made plainer. He is idiosyncratically humane and rational and his radicalism is directed at the reduction of inhumanity and irrationalism. It has no other parameters.

He sums up his own beliefs through an allusion to a passage from David Hume:

that it is a sense of shared humanity and that alone which can provide the basis for civilized existence: though this affection of humanity may

*See p. 18 for discussion of Boyle's acceptance of positive discrimination in education.

†Conversation with Anthony Crosland, April 1971. See also his defence of 'labour populism' as against 'Liberal progressivism' in the *Sunday Times*, 4 April 1971.

not generally be esteemed so strongly as vanity or ambition, yet being common to all men it can alone be the foundation of morals or any general system of blame or praise.'[3]

The eclecticism is explicit:

While admitting the political danger of the sophisticated doubter, I do not think that all questions should be prejudged. Society can do with a certain amount of cross-grain in theory; such as Conservatives who don't like capital punishment and Socialists who don't like comprehensive schools.[4]

I remember Robert Nield saying to me 'I always feel that with you, you are looking for the value-judgement as the joker in the pack' ... I've never been somebody who has found it easy to conceive that there could be a sort of norm of right thinking (see p. 74).*

He said as much to his own Party Conference in 1968:

I will join with you in the fight against Socialist dogmatism wherever it rears its head. But do not ask me to oppose it with an equal or opposite Conservative dogmatism, because in education it is the dogmatism itself which is wrong.

Because he was free of rigid moralistic commitments he found it easy to meet the social radicalism of the 1960s half way. In 1962 he said, 'One of the most important aspects in the educational system is to try to compensate for the inequality of home environment of children over the country' – a commitment echoed in his foreword to the *Newsom Report* in 1963.[5] This stated 'the essential point is that all children should have an equal opportunity of acquiring intelligence, and developing their talents and abilities to the full.'† This has been rightly remarked as 'a milestone in Conservative thinking'.[6] Hence his sponsoring of 'positive discrimination' implicit in the *Plowden Report*,[7] which other Conservatives, such as Timothy Raison, a member of the Plowden Committee and now a conservative MP, found no difficulty in endorsing.‡

*At this point in time Robert Nield was in the Economic Division of the Treasury.

†Boyle confesses (p. 93) to being uncertain as to the origin of this dictum. In fact, it appeared first in Anthony Crosland's *The Conservative Enemy*, Cape, 1962.

‡At the time of his membership of the Plowden Committee, Timothy Raison was editor of *New Society*.

The bewilderment remains and is not helped by those who explain Boyle as 'a man . . . so deeply . . . Conservative that he can afford to entertain progressive ideas without any anxiety that they will weaken the main structure of his political beliefs'.[8] He is not 'deeply Conservative' but deeply agnostic and eclectic. That somewhat over-anxious organ of Conservative opinion, the *Daily Telegraph*, was nearer the truth when it demanded that 'Sir Edward Boyle's prolonged flirtation with both selectivity and comprehensivization must end: the two are incompatible'.[9] While positive discrimination can be argued by those who assert opportunity as well as those who assert equality, selection cannot coexist with comprehensive education.

Boyle's willingness to regard arguments as open, rather than his ability to conclude them, was one of his contributions to Ministerial style. He declared no clear programme to which his supporters could rally, other than expansionism so as to increase opportunity, and free expression – as with his defence of his Principal Medical Officer's right to state his own views on pre-marital sex. At a time when images rather than subtle principles, simple propositions rather than subtle Humeism, pull in the votes, this could never be a political advantage.

Crosland, too, was explicit about his values but was more clear about what programmes would promote them best. His *The Future of Socialism* has appealed to an audience far wider than those interested in the particular causes it advances.[10] In Halsey's view Crosland, in this book, established education 'as a serious alternative to nationalization in promoting a more just and efficient society'.[11] This argument was strategic in converting the Labour Party away from the flat-cap adherence to Clause Four of its Constitution and reinforcing Gaitskell's, and the party's, acceptance of a mixed, but controlled, economy. Crosland continues to be the single theorist of Cabinet calibre who can also act effectively as a Minister.

The book also argued that 'as an investment, education yields a generous return: we badly need more of it in Britain'. Crosland argued, then, both on grounds of economic investment and of social justice, years before getting office, for better education services, an end to selectivity and to 'the more glaring injustice of the public schools'.

Neither men were party conformists and both helped to change their traditional party doctrines – Crosland on nationalization and Boyle on attitudes towards expanding the social services. But the difference in their party allegiances produced differences in the pressure on them. Boyle was under pressure not to yield to demands for an end to selectivity from the predominantly Labour cities. Crosland had to defend himself from those who, on the public schools, on the pace of comprehensivization, on the organization of higher education, wanted to eradicate divisiveness quickly – and all with a dwindling Labour majority of six.*

Boyle was a reluctant Conservative and Crosland a cautious revolutionary. Both were beneficiaries of the popular mood of the 1960s when few were prepared to argue against stronger government leadership and intervention in education.

Their personal commitments must be seen against a background of several related themes in post-war educational history. Firstly, the recognition that spending on education is investment as well as consumption. Secondly, the reinforcement of earlier arguments from social compassion for educational improvement so as to redress maldistribution of benefits. Thirdly, the acceptance that providing more education meets, and ought to meet, increasingly strong social demand. Fourthly, the conflict between the assumptions of pre-war educational psychology and the post-war radical sociologists about the extent to which ability could be reliably predicted. Fifthly, the ideological conflicts between those who wanted selective and those who wanted non-selective education. And, finally, the way in which the public debate on these themes affected the changing role of central government.

David Eccles,† as can be seen in his 1956 White Paper on technical education, was the first Minister to assume that educational expenditure was economic investment.[12] The same

*Until the April 1966 General Election produced a Labour majority of 97.
†Now Viscount Eccles, Minister of Education, 1954–7, and again 1959–62, and Minister of State for Education since June 1970.

assumptions were later to be deployed in the *Crowther Report*'s assessment of the case for raising the school-leaving age.[13] The Plowden Committee attempted to formulate – but its task was more difficult – similar arguments for improvements in primary education.[14] These arguments had been advanced first by economists in the USA and then, following the lead given by John Vaizey, in the UK.

The earlier arguments for increased educational investment had a different source – social compassion. Both the *Hadow Report* and R. H. Tawney used exactly the same words: 'What a wise and good parent will desire for his own children, a nation must desire for all children'.[15] Tawney was a member of the Hadow Committee. That the economic arguments are still not concluded is reflected in the doubts expressed by Maudling, as Chancellor of the Exchequer (see p. 118). And the ways in which education might or might not affect economic growth are still being argued by Vaizey, Blaug and many others.

Though they may have merit in themselves, arguments from economic growth can also support the more fundamental, and politically viable, arguments of social demand – the pressure for places first created by increasing waves of population growth which hit the education service successively from the late 1940s onwards. Then there were the demands of those within the service for a longer period of compulsory schooling and for a longer period of teacher training, which gave impetus to yet another set of demands for more further education and more university places.

Each year in the 1950s and the 1960s increased numbers, and an increased proportion of each age group, successfully took GCE O and A levels and thus furnished the bases for predictions of demand which so influenced the Robbins estimates – now shown by present student enrolments to be far too conservative.[16] The people were thus voting with their feet for educational expansion. The newspapers of the early 1950s, particularly the local papers of the commuter belt, were full of tales of woe at increased educational spending, at the creation of 'glass palaces', of schools with twelve acres of playing fields. In the late 1950s opinion moved decisively towards education as desirable both for its own sake and as a way by which individuals could furnish themselves with necessary skills. Education has proved one of the consumer durables for which the market has opted. And it was largely Eccles and Boyle who legitimized – indeed stimulated – these demands.

Social demand for more education required no stronger ideology than individual self-interest. The growing attacks on divisiveness in the system, on ways in which it differentiated children, were a slower and more complex development. In 1967, 53 per cent of parents wanted their child to go to grammar or independent schools, 52 per cent were in favour of comprehensive education, while 76 per cent were in favour of retaining grammar schools,[17] confirmation, perhaps, of Wilson's double-think dictum that all children should have a grammar-school education.

The education system, and Ministers who presided over it, were, in fact, encountering not only the uncertainties and anxieties felt by individual parents about the educational future of their children but, more fundamentally, the uncertainties about social stratification in Great Britain first generated in the 1940s. For the first time, in the late 1940s, grammar school boys were going to Oxbridge on full subsistence grants, given as a legal duty by the Ministry, or by the local education authorities. They, too, were having their shoes cleaned at public expense by scouts and gyps and bedders. The war had lent social mobility a sudden, if episodic, momentum. It gave commissions to, and made gentlemen of, those who might otherwise have been hidden in the middle or lower ranks of local government service or the retail trade or large joint stock banks. After the war, the growth of credit facilities, the spread of the BBC culture – both aural and oral – increasingly available travel abroad, the flood of paperback books, the unfreezing of social relations, induced by some of the policies of the great post-war Labour government, uncertainty about who one was and what one might become, affected the intellectual and political climate, and, with it, assumptions about education. If cockneys could make millions by selling scrap iron, if Herbert Morrison or Ernest Bevin – who both left school at the age of twelve – could be the second and third Ministers of the nation, how could some measurement experts claim to identify the nation's talent by setting a test to eleven year olds?

Increasingly, popular intuition followed the advice of three expert witnesses to the Plowden Committee, that it is unsafe to predict a man's future before the age of forty.*

Intelligence testing had expertly and convincingly claimed to detect 'general ability' (G factor) and it reached, in Great Britain, a high state of technical competence. It was adopted not to reduce the chances of working-class children, but to improve them. It was intended to reinforce the egalitarian doctrines of the 1920s, 1930s and 1940s by enabling the abilities of the underprivileged to be identified and nourished. It was, in fact, a device to help establish the Opportunity State. And it thus shored up what Anthony Crosland labelled the 'weak concept of equality' (see p. 51).

The doctrine became official in such phrases as those of the Education Act: 'education according to age, ability and aptitude' (the distinction between the latter two categories was not made all that clear) which were to replace a system which provided education according to means. On it was founded the doctrine of 'secondary education for all' in which 'parity of esteem' between different types of secondary education was to be maintained. In form at least, it was a promise handsomely kept – excellent new buildings for secondary modern schools were built, for example.

The attacks on the weak or opportunity concept of equality came from many quarters. First, psychologists such as Philip Vernon and Torsten Husén of Stockholm threw doubt on the reliability and validity of testing. The reliability of testing over time was poor.† Children's ability had been shown to shift with opportunity. The system's judgements on pupils created the future that they predicted – once in a secondary modern school, the bright child behaved according to the expectation

*Philip Vernon, W. D. Wall and Gilbert Peaker (oral, unpublished evidence).

†This literature is succinctly summarized in the *Plowden Report*, ch. 2, paras. 56–64, '. . . if the I Q had been made the single criterion at nine or ten for sorting the children into sheep or goats, and if the same criterion had been used again at nineteen, it would have been found that a mistake had been made in 20 per cent of the cases' (para. 59).

of the secondary modern school rather than to the expectation of the secondary grammar school that he never knew.

At the same time, sociologists had taken stock of the system as a distributor of social rights. The famous succession of official and other reports, *Early Leaving,* Crowther, Newsom, Robbins, Plowden, and Douglas,[18] showed that access to the more favoured forms of education was differentiated according to social class. Floud, Halsey and Martin showed how the creation of free places for grammar schools benefitted the middle rather than the lower socio-economic classes.[19] And the mechanics of social differentiation – different codes of language learned in the cradle – began to be held up for scrutiny by Basil Bernstein in 1961 in his celebrated article 'Social class and linguistic development'.[20]

The intelligentsia thus provided the data and the arguments upon which the CAC (Central Advisory Council) Reports, drafted by those who saw the impact of the system largely from the viewpoint of the schools, could feed. The first official admission that the opportunity doctrines of the 1944 Act were adrift came from Edward Boyle in his preface to Newsom already quoted.

Boyle summarizes the ideological process as being the

two traditions in the Department: the social justice tradition, wanting to widen opportunity, giving people the greater opportunity to acquire intelligence, and the technical college tradition – education for investment, education for efficiency. They were described in the early 1960s, rather happily I thought, by Toby Weaver, as 'the dialectic within the office' – and that dialectic was quite sharp.* Twenty years earlier the dialectic would have been thought inappropriate to the Board of Education anyway (see p. 123).

The changes in popular ideology – towards expansionism, first to increase opportunity and then to create equality – made the different tasks of the two radical Ministers easier. They were both able to confirm and to advance the ideologies already in the air when they came into office. These changes

*Deputy Under-Secretary of State, DES, from 1962 to the present. Weaver is now responsible for higher education. Previously he was Under-Secretary, Schools Branch (from 1956), and has thus occupied strategic positions in all main aspects of educational policy for nearly twenty years.

in ideology also affected the role of the centre, which became stronger under the demands of the etatist doctrine that there should be more public education provision.

The Changing Role of the Department

Against the general movement of ideas in the 1960s – which reinforced the role of the centre – and the personal and political beliefs of the two Ministers, it is possible to examine the authority and power that Crosland and Boyle wielded, and to see how their roles related to the whole system of educational government.

The Secretary of State for Education and Science* mainly mediates his authority through a system of controls, duties and powers which puts him in relationship with 169 local education authorities.†

Yet another part of the system – we shall not review it all – is mediated through relationships between the Secretary of State and the universities.‡ This relationship is largely, but not wholly, carried out through the University Grants Committee which he appoints, and which formally recommends the grants to be made by the DES.

The Minister's relationship with local authorities is stated with more grandiloquence than precision in Section 1 of the Education Act, 1944.** He has the duty

---

*Crosland and Boyle were Ministers in charge of the English and Welsh education systems. Scotland and Northern Ireland had their own system of educational government and their own Ministers. Welsh education is now under the Secretary of State for Wales.

†This is the present number of English and Welsh local educational authorities. For part of the time that Boyle was in office (before the London Government Act, 1963, was passed) there were 169 LEAs. The number will be again reduced if the proposals in the present government's White Paper on local government reorganization (HMSO, Cmnd. 4584) become law. The local authorities are the councils of the counties and county boroughs. They delegate most of their authority to education committees which they are required by statute to appoint.

‡By Anthony Crosland's time the Secretary of State was also responsible for science. It was agreed, in the interviews, not to consider the relationships resulting from that responsibility.

**This strong statement of the new Ministry's role was backed up by the President of the Board of Education, R. A. Butler, in taking the Bill through the Commons. He said that the government 'should lead boldly'. The *White*

to promote the education of the people of England and Wales and the progressive development of institutions devoted to that purpose and to *secure the effective execution by the local educational authorities under his control and direction of the national policy* for providing a varied and comprehensive educational service in every area [my italics].

The detailed sections of the Act, however, place strong provisos against this somewhat etatist declaration.

Section 23 of the Act, for example, places the decision on the content of the curriculum firmly with local authorities and school governors (except the legal insistence on religious education and the act of worship) rather than with the Department. The Secretary of State's controls over the allocation if not the supply of teachers to local authorities, and over building programmes, are based on legally tenuous foundations. But even where powers are not explicit, the conventions are that Ministers exercise authority not plainly written in law, conventions reinforced by the knowledge that if a Secretary of State so wishes, he can get what legal power he needs to implement policies.

Many powers are, of course, explicit. The power to approve the establishment, closure or change in size or scope of a school under Section 13 of the Act, for example, enables the Department to control local authority plans for school reorganization and – more important in the past than now – to control the balance between local authority and denominationally provided schools. At almost every point in the system the Education Acts give the Secretary of State the right to dispose of *changes* in provision.

National policies strongly prescribe what a local authority can do: the length of compulsory school life, the salaries paid to teachers,* minimum building standards and maximum build-

---

Paper on Educational Reconstruction (HMSO, Cmd. 6458, 1943) which preceded the Act emphasized that 'the public system of education, though administered locally, is the nation's concern' and 'the full benefits should be equally available to all alike, wherever their homes may be'.

*Salaries are decided by the Burnham Committee on which local authorities, teacher organizations and government are represented. Government can, in effect, veto a Burnham decision. The DES administers Burnham decisions by interpreting them to the LEAs which employ, appoint and pay the teachers.

ing costs, pupil–teacher ratios are administered by authorities within nationally prescribed limits. A local education and finance committee exercises discretion within limits prescribed as much in Curzon Street as in County Hall. And local authorities, despite the promises of the Local Government Act, 1958 (which introduced the general grant ostensibly to increase authorities' freedom) and the later arguments of first the Herbert and later the Maud Commission,[21] have increasingly yielded authority to the centre on the most important issues. Furthermore, local government finance is dependent upon the rate support grants made available for almost all local authority services by government. The range and level, but not the style and quality, of local authorities' activities are thus largely prescribed by central government.

Yet local authorities are reckoned to be free bodies, relating as much to local electors' wishes as to national policy. There is, however, no necessary conflict between local authorities' freedom and the DES's strong control functions. Prescriptive limits can be the boundaries of wide and strong use of discretion. Legislation is proposed or, in effect, made by Ministers working through Parliament and it confers on the local authorities powers and duties. The results of this freedom are real and striking; they can be seen less in the obvious indicators of performance – levels of education of teachers, quality of buildings, performance in public secondary examinations – than in the style of education (formal or informal), of buildings (traditional plan or modern free-flow), of relations between teachers and administration. American visitors admire, and now try to imitate, this combination of a strong national role and local freedom.

If the role of the centre has always been strong, it has become stronger. Traditionally, the controls were regulatory and quasi-judicial. Some of the finest essays in the language were and are written by civil servants and hidden on DES files – judicious, even reflective, discussions and timeless constructions of citizens' rights and public authorities' duties, rather than proposals for direct action; on the right of parents to choose their children's schools, on whether a school's swimming-pool is a building or part of the playing-fields, on the regulation of financial arrangements between the denominations and the centre and local authorities.

The role and the style of the centre have changed with current ideologies. The philosophy of those administering, as Ministers, administrators or as HMIs, the new democracy of the 1944 Act, its Whiggish character – 'secondary education for all' but 'according to age, ability and aptitude' – were different from the ideology of the preceding era. This had accepted the all-age and senior elementary schools* whose pupils had no purchase on the moving staircase of social mobility; a society in which the mass of children left school, still children, at fourteen; the frustrations of the able underprivileged only too glad to get an education in stuffily pseudoclassic grammar schools – and nothing more. And like good Aristotelians, the policy makers in Curzon Street in the late 1940s and early 1950s were rational, compassionate and logical. But, no Minister, Labour or Tory, had asked them to specify the objectives of the educational system, let alone to specify how life-chances might be related to educational benefit. No one had invented, let alone made them face up to, the language of indicative planning. This had to wait the like of Gösta Rehn of Sweden in whose veins, one observer noted, the ink freely runs.† No one had told them to be on guard against the alchemy of the educational psychologists, or to question local authority testing procedures. So officials (I was one of them) dutifully wrote to aggrieved parents of children who had failed the 11-plus – an exam over which the Ministry had no control – that they had been tested by means that would detect their true ability, untainted by cultural factors. Such expressions as 'secondary education for all', 'parity of esteem' were thought to be radical if not revolutionary doctrines – Menshevik rather than Bolshevik, yet not at all out of

*The senior elementary schools have some stalwart and knowledgeable defenders. See Lionel Elvin's essay in R. S. Peters (ed.), *Perspectives on Plowden*, Routledge & Kegan Paul, 1969. One distinguished former H M I recently told the author that some pre-war senior elementary schools were among the best he had ever seen. He would agree, however, that this did not establish access for their pupils to higher education or the professions.

†Rehn is now Director, Manpower and Social Affairs, O E C D.

line with the scientific judgements of the educational psychologists.

Nor did the Ministry test the technological assumptions behind the weak concept of equality. It had expertise in the HM
Inspectorate but not, as yet, access to a social science intelligentsia. And it was still nervous about touching any issue that
could be called 'educational'.

In the 1950s several changes occured which decisively altered
the balance of power between central and local government.
First, the need for more effective economic control produced
two of the best examples of creative and knowledgeable
administration that the Welfare State displays: the creation
of the Department's Architects and Building Branch, and
of control and predictive mechanisms for teacher supply,
the Teacher Supply Branch. The Department's Architects
and Building Branch showed how central government could
give leadership in an area where resource control and design
development converge. It showed, too, that central government could, if it gave its mind to it, find the resources and use
some of its best talents for development work. The early
efforts of such local authorities as Hertfordshire, where the
Chief Education Officer, John Newsom,* was said to go about
the country with a trumpet in one hand and a trowel in the
other creating imaginative but economic school buildings,
were taken up by the appointment of the county architect,
Stirrat Johnson-Marshall, as chief architect to the Ministry.
He started in joint headship of the new Branch with a succession of creative administrators: Antony Part, David Nenk,
Derek Morrell, Bill Pile and John Hudson.† The Department

*Sir John Newsom later became Chairman of the Central Advisory
Council for Education and of the Public Schools Commission. He died in
May 1971.

†Of these, Nenk and Morrell died as young Under-Secretaries, but are
already part of British administrative hagiology. David Nenk became
Under-Secretary, Finance and Accountant-General, Minister of Education.
Derek Morrell was, at his death in 1969, Assistant Under-Secretary of State
in charge of the Children's Department, Home Office. He was commonly
reckoned to be the driving force behind the Schools Council and the drafting
of the Children and Young Persons Act, 1969. *New Society* described him
(18 December 1969) as 'one of the great reformers in the government'.
Antony Part is now Permanent Under-Secretary of State, Department of

thus found itself drawn into the essentials of the education process because building development requires definition of function, though it was undoubtedly also drawn by the lure of savings and design for function.

The nightmare of teacher maldistribution caused Eccles to apply, after consultation, a 'voluntary' quota on teachers, administered by a centrally devised and administered system through the Teacher Supply Branch – a manpower planning unit, in effect.

These two moves brought the Department from being the holder of the ring between the 'real' forces in educational policy making, which had hitherto been the local authorities, the denominations, and the teachers and parents, to being the enforcer of positive controls, based increasingly on knowledge which the Department itself went out to get. What Boyle eloquently called 'the economics of Passchendaele' forced the Department into strategic planning. Yet whenever called upon to pronounce, central government dutifully preached the contrary to central control. Crosland says, frankly, that all who have had to cope with local government are schizophrenic about the extent of central government's control over it (see p. 171).

To be interested, however, in manpower distribution, or building costs, is still in linear descent from Gladstone's interest in saving candle ends. There was significant change in this, but the real innovation of these years was that Ministers were increasingly prepared to test, and to promote, value-led assumptions on the purposes as well as the control of the system.

Because Ministers have chosen, and local authorities have naturally reinforced their choice, not to wield all of the authority they possess, two consequences have resulted. First, there is remarkable, and beneficial, variety in British education, as compared with, say, France. Secondly, Ministers cannot carry through policies simply by virtue of clear thinking. They have to carry the system with them. Both Boyle and Crosland saw this and were good at it (see pp. 125 and 173).

Trade and Industry. William Pile is Permanent Under-Secretary of State, D E S, where John Hudson is a Deputy Secretary.

Their ability to run the system also, however, depended on their relationship with the rest of the government system.

The Minister as Manager

While both former Ministers believe that central government should create objectives, both disclaim any direct managerial role in running the education service.* This disclaimer needs to be tested.

If local authorities are really acting under Ministers' direction and control, it must be assumed Ministers set explicit objectives for the service, that they are accountable for their achievement, and that they have authority to see they are achieved.

First, both Ministers justifiably claim that they knew what their objectives were (see pp. 103 and 152). One, the Conservative, was concerned that the opportunity state should become real and that education should improve freedom of choice; Crosland was concerned with a more positive reversal of deprivation and had far more radical objections to a divisive system.

Both of these policies are apposite to the role of a Minister. They are the sort of judgement that we elect our politicians to make. Both were actualized in decisions on the organization of secondary education made by Ministers under Section 13 of the Education Act, 1944, in decisions on the rate of spending allowed to local authorities, in decisions on the school leaving age, on the scale and structure of higher education, and so on.

Crosland must have been concerned to make his objectives more manifest and active in his administration when he established the Planning Branch in the Department of Education and Science. He was not there long enough to guarantee the Branch adequate status in relationship to other branches of the Department. Its weakness was, as Crosland implies in one

*Earlier, Lord Hailsham, on becoming Minister, remarked: 'In the Admiralty you are a person having authority. You say to one person "Come" and he cometh, and another "Go" and he goeth. It is not so in the Ministry of Education. You suggest rather than direct. You say to one man "Come" and he cometh not and to another "Go" and he stays where he is.'

of his more guarded answers, perhaps the result of official resistance to the Branch in the first place (see p. 183). Boyle, clear minded as he was, had not yet got to the stage of thinking in terms of such machinery when he was Minister. The 'objectives' game had only just crossed the Atlantic and the Channel, and is now brought to us perhaps more by the management consultants and the output budgeting pundits than by our political leaders. These are Ministers of the 1960s. They were some steps behind, say, Robert MacNamara in the US Department of Defense, Edward Heath's White Paper, *The Reorganization of Central Government*[22] – with its emphasis on objectives and its creation of a Capability Unit for their articulation – may mark a turning point in Britain's administrative history – though Crosland expressed many doubts in the Commons debate about it.*

But if involved in the statement of objectives, was the Secretary of State also accountable for their pursuit in the education service? Both Boyle and Crosland accept in these conversations the conventional wisdom that control of the schools should rest with the local education authorities and the institutions themselves. They would reserve to the centre the establishment of major policies, resting on the values established by Ministers. At this point in the discussion we have problems of definition. How do we define the role of the Minister in charge of the armed services, or the Minister in charge of the hospitals (which are governed by boards and committees appointed by him using funds made available to him) and distinguish it from the role of the Minister charged with

*3 November 1970. 'Given that, at the end of the day, almost all of these judgements are political and a matter of political values, I think that it is much better that the initial appraisal should be carried out by officials directly responsible to the Minister and not by this roving group of outside businessmen with their vague position in the Cabinet Office.' He agreed that there was room for improvement in the control of public expenditure but doubted whether improvement could come from 'this group of businessmen who will no doubt be doing programme budgeting in all directions'. And, 'It is ironic that the enthusiasm stirred up for programme budgeting by the hon. member for Guildford [David Howell – a Parliamentary Secretary to the Treasury concerned with the civil service matters, under the Prime Minister] and others should coincide with a growing scepticism on the subject in the US and indeed a certain retreat from it.'

'the control and direction of the education service'? Ostensibly they are three very different roles in charge of different
governing systems. But are they? Ministers are listened to by
the education service because they have authority to make
decisions which affect organizational behaviour. They may
also be listened to because of charismatic force. But there are
other equally charismatic spokesmen who lack authority.
Ministers of Education have no alibis, even if authority is
partly in the hands of local authorities. Their decisions affect
activities – their purpose and level of performance – throughout the service. They do not have the managerial style of, say,
the Chairman of British Rail. They are powerful interpos-
itions in the lines of authority and accountability – the elected local authorities, the acknowledged freedom (but not
autonomy) of the schools. Neither Boyle or Crosland would
think it correct factually or appropriate politically to assert
the position of Minister as manager. Certainly, a local authority can build its schools – or wreck its town centre – according to its own tastes. But it is difficult to differentiate one
type of Ministerial role from the other stronger roles.

Yet the Secretary of State has authority over the work of
local education authorities. Thus, it was thought bizarre, but
not inconsistent with his role, that Sir David Eccles should
answer a Parliamentary question about a school playground
over which a hunt had chased a fox ('Neither the fox nor the
hunt sought the permission of the school authorities', he replied). MPs write to Ministers about the minutiae of local
authority administration – about a school which forced a
child to finish his school dinner. There have also been a few
cases since the war when the Minister has directed a local
authority to stop acting 'unreasonably'. But where are the
determinant decisions taken? While local control over curriculum and appointment of teachers affects radically the style
of the service given, so many of the decisions – the rate of
building, the number of teachers permitted, the sizes of classes,
the length of school life, the whole structure of higher, and
most recently secondary, education – are subjects of central
policy that it is virtually impossible to detect *real* differences
in the relationships between the Secretary of State for Health

and the regional hospital boards that he appoints and the relationships between the Secretary of State for Education and
the local education authorities that the electors appoint. But
central government is not prepared to recognize the fact that
its own role is ambivalent, that it has a yo-yo relationship
with local government. So there is obviously uncertainty as
to whether the Minister is *accountable* for the schools in the
same way as one Secretary of State is for the army, or another
for the hospitals. Thus Crosland:

There is in no sense a single organization with a managerial chain of
command. On the other hand, I was very much struck by how much
influence, control, power . . . the Department has (see p. 169).

Perhaps better leave it at that. The role of central government is poorly defined and the best descriptions of central–
local government relationships seem to do no more than describe ambivalences.[23]

Ministers and the Machinery of Government

Ministers of Education have to relate their decision making
to that of the Prime Minister, the Cabinet, the Treasury and
others at the apex of the government machine. The relationships between these roles are explained in some of the answers
given by Crosland and Boyle. But we must not generalize from
Education to the whole of government. Crosland emphasizes
the differences between Education and Trade (see p. 162). Boyle
thinks that a few Departments – Education and Agriculture –
need Ministers who will champion their service, because they
more than most must always fight for resources. 'There always
had to be an element of the anti-government about the Ministry of Education' (see p. 142). Education emerges as a somewhat lonely, if important, vice-royalty – perhaps the Welfare
State equivalent of imperial Britain's India. Yet some general-
izations about the whole machine can be made.

The controversy over whether we have Cabinet or Prime
Ministerial government[24] might be resolved by applying two
criteria. First, who takes the main decisions affecting the
education service – Prime Minister or Cabinet or Secretary of

State? And second, who has authority to make these decisions stick?

Boyle attributes support for the Act enabling middle schools to be created to Home (see p. 78) – apart from this, the Prime Minister does not emerge as a determiner of his policies. Crosland observes that 'When he moved me to the Board of Trade, he [Harold Wilson] remarked on the fact that he hadn't once had a conversation with me about education.' But this evidence does not conclusively define the relationship. Non-intervention by the Prime Minister might mean that he feels education to be unimportant, or important but competently handled – as Crosland was surely entitled to assume (see p. 160).

A better indication is not what Macmillan or Wilson did, but what they could do. The Prime Minister appoints and can remove Ministers. Crosland and Boyle moved into and out of Education, at the Prime Minister's behest, with somewhat more rapidity than would, say, a manager move into a bank or a supermarket. This authority to appoint, transfer and dismiss enables the Prime Minister to allocate values and thus change or confirm an individual Minister's policies. Thus, Churchill's decision to replace Horsburgh by Eccles, or Wilson's removal of Gordon Walker, are constructable as Prime Ministerial judgements about the style and quality of leadership that the Prime Minister wished to attribute to the education service. So were Macmillan's and Wilson's decisions to leave Boyle and Crosland to get on with it. Other major issues – whether there should be one or two Ministers of Education – are reserved to the Prime Minister because of the convention that the Cabinet has no concern with Ministerial appointments (see p. 105). He can thus not only appoint and dismiss but also shape areas of responsibility, as with the decisions taken by Home to combine Education and Science.

These elements of authority make the Prime Minister a Minister's manager, and give him ultimate authority over educational government.* And notice, too, the dependence –

*The opposite point of view is well argued by A. Brown, 'What power has the Prime Minister?', *New Society*, 1 June 1967. 'There is a world of perhaps a matter of personal style and allegiance – of Boyle's on the Prime Minister's approval.

I raised this matter with my Cabinet colleagues before the end of July. Mr Macmillan told me afterwards he thought I presented it quite sensibly (see p. 81).

Not quite the language of an equal responding to the judgement of his peer.

If the Prime Minister is the manager of other Ministers, the Cabinet cannot be the supreme point in government. Nor is it a meeting of equals acting in coalition.* It is rather a meeting of departmental heads taking decisions in collective form under the eye of a common manager who can, and does, assess individual Ministers' competence through their contribution (including their ability to keep quiet) to Cabinet proceedings.

If the Prime Minister, in effect, has this control over the Cabinet, this does not of itself leave the Cabinet with no authority. As Boyle puts it, 'Cabinet decisions ... are the most important directions of all that Permanent Secretaries can get' (p. 111). The point is that Cabinet decisions are made by those who depend for their appointment and support for their policies on the Prime Minister. If the Prime Minister dislikes the decisions made by the Cabinet, he can change the Cabinet. This is not to say that Prime Ministers do not depend on their colleagues' support. Prime Ministers (e.g. Asquith) have been removed by the action of their colleagues. His *authority* depends on the *power* he commands. But the Prime Minister has supreme authority while in office; when this begins to go, the Prime Minister is about to go as well.

Granted that the Cabinet, under its Prime Minister manager, has authority, what decisions does it take? Crosland and Boyle submitted few issues to it. Overall decisions on public expenditure are taken by Cabinet. Specifically educational issues are rarely seen. For example, Crosland submitted only his circular on comprehensive schools and his appointment of the Public

---

difference between choosing Ministers and dictating to them.' But no sensible manager 'dictates'. The issue is not one of style but of the structural relationships affected by the Prime Minister's authority.

*Patrick Gordon Walker argues this view. See p. 61, n. 24.

Schools Commission. The Cabinet obviously does not scan all of the policies for which it allegedly takes collective responsibility* – how can it? – and is plainly *not* 'the mainspring of all the mechanism of government'.[25] As Crosland puts it: 'if a Minister is not capable of being his own mainspring and initiating his own policies he should be sacked. Not, alas, that he always is . . .' (p. 163).

Ministers themselves decide what to take to the Cabinet, though the Secretary to the Cabinet effectively determines the agenda, acting on the Prime Minister's behalf (see p. 108). Many more issues are decided by reference to Cabinet Committees – Crosland quotes as an example the government's decision on how to treat the Maud Commission's recommendations on local government reorganization (p. 169).

Some issues – foreign policy, defence, economics – come automatically to the Cabinet. And many of them are of both immediate and long-term importance. But long-term importance is not a leading criterion. Thus Boyle:

. . . any Minister who tried to get real interest in something that didn't involve a decision on expenditure, was a long-term issue but not one on the accepted agenda, at any given moment, would be more likely to meet bored acquiescence from his colleagues, rather than active agreement (p. 109).

Or:

. . . how often we would get on to something quite important at ten to one and would settle that by one o'clock. One or two decisions did come up which we settled in Cabinet in ten minutes, and I think somebody ought to have said 'Look, this really is rather important, and, whoever's right or wrong about this, I think we ought to give careful thought to it before reaching a conclusion' . . . (p. 96).

Again, in Crosland's words:

There isn't much correlation between how important an issue is and how much time is spent on this in Cabinet . . . The issues that take up Cabinet time are those which are controversial within the government . . . It's not their intrinsic importance, but their political content, that puts them on the Cabinet agenda (p. 161).

*This doctrine is flaking too. Cabinets are, for example, informed of the contents of a Chancellor's budget speech the day or morning before it is delivered in the House. Decisions on bank rate or, for that matter, on the Suez affair are not submitted for Cabinet approval.

The Cabinet can make or break a policy. But both Ministers make it plain that the individual Minister of Education rather than the Cabinet is the focal point of political initiatives and decisions in education, perhaps because, as Crosland puts it, 'They thought it was going quite well and I was carrying out party policy' (p. 161). But if this is so, it means that once a party is in office, Ministers are so busy carrying out agreed policies in their own zones, that they are not able to create new policies *collectively*. It makes the period of opposition critically important to the process of policy fashioning. In the social services, at least, years are fruitful or wasted as much in opposition as in government.*

Thus it is to the Ministers in the Department, working through the administrative networks with other Departments, that we must look for the loci of educational policy making. The Cabinet is a somewhat remote point of last resort.

If the role of the Cabinet has been overstated, both Ministers confirm a commonplace of British government – the Treasury's decisive say in educational and all policy making. If, as Boyle puts it, the DES is the 'sponsoring Department' for its service, the Treasury is the Department which clinches all but the most important proposals the DES sponsors. The difficulty, again, is defining rather than describing its role.

It seems to me† that the Treasury, until recently, had four roles.‡ It controlled the economy, and had operational functions similar to those of the DES for Education or the DHSS for Health – though obviously, the nature of the control was different. This made it a Department with its own sectional

---

*This point is obviously well taken by Anthony Crosland who has always used periods of opposition to systematically examine party politics against new thinking in the social services. No other senior Labour Minister has produced books on policy of the importance of those listed on p. 60, n. 10, and he has been quick to get on with it since June 1970.

†But Crosland has a somewhat different view: see p. 168.

‡Wilson removed management of the civil service to the Civil Service Department as a result of the *Fulton Report*'s recommendations. The Treasury's role has also been challenged by Heath's creation of the Capability Unit in the Cabinet Office, reporting directly to the Prime Minister.

interests competing with every other Department – there is room for choice between, say, an export boom, with all of its costs, and a boom in school or hospital building. It also had a *staff* role – financial collation and control of *all* government activity. That is to say, if the Prime Minister and Cabinet decided, with the Departmental Ministers, what policies to pursue, the Treasury would advise on the financial consequences, and, once a decision was taken, police the financial controls embodying that decision. Crosland is illuminating about the process of financial control and macro-economic policy making (p. 168). Thirdly, it had another staff role – personnel and organizational advice and control again affecting all government and much other public organization And, finally, it was, as the Civil Service Commission used to describe it, 'the central organ of government'.[26] In my view there was, and still is, a hopeless confusion of roles, so that the staff authority over finance is used to control policy initiatives from other Departments, and to overrate economic management.[27]

Boyle, however, gives the Treasury credit for knowing where its role ought to have begun and ended (see p. 113). The Treasury were cautious, he thought, about impinging on the rights of the DES to decide educational objectives. A Treasury official would establish the best methods of controlling educational expenditure – apparently by restraining capital investment – but be less concerned about choices between different forms of educational expenditure, unless there were such a clear economic basis of choice as a preference for further education, for example. But this example, which Boyle quotes, precisely demonstrates how the Treasury's economic policy making is backed up by its financial control authority.

It is interesting to see how these two strong Ministers accepted as inevitable the decisive part that Treasury officials play in determining the success or otherwise of their policies.

The Minister and his Department

'Ministers . . . belong to a party as well as a government and they are appointed with the responsibility of making clear what their value-judgements are.' Crosland endorses Boyle's judgement that this – the authoritative enunciation of values – is the essential element of the Ministerial role (see pp. 74 and 153). But how do these value-judgements enter the blood stream of the Department?

Take the realities of the Ministry of Education when Boyle first came to it. There was one Minister and one Parliamentary Secretary. The administrative-class staff consisted of a Permanent Secretary (who had begun in the Ministry in the 1920s) and a Deputy Secretary who began in the late 1930s and had, in fact, drafted the 1944 Act. There were six Under-Secretaries and perhaps twenty Assistant Secretaries. There were twenty-five to thirty Principals. And there were about five hundred HMIs – mainly a selected group of former teachers.

Decisions were of two main types. There were decisions on cases referred to the Ministry – such as a proposal of a local authority to extend a school, or a decision to confirm a compulsory purchase order (decisions later reserved for Ministers), or a decision on whether to press a local authority on an appeal from an aggrieved parent. Such decisions were largely taken by Principals, or their subordinates, within general policies. But a second class of decision – on the main themes of policy – was brought up in a succession of memoranda and meetings that could start with a Principal or higher and might or might not finish, or start, with Ministers. The system flexibly allowed decisions of virtually any importance, or of whatever value content – policy or the minute application of policy through case decisions – to be taken at any of the levels. A Minister could choose to spend hours on the minutiae of a reorganization scheme before allowing a Principal to sign a letter formally approving the proposal under Section 13 of the Education Act, 1944. Or an Under-Secretary could propose in a meeting of other Under-Secretaries that local government's grants from central government should take the form of general rather than of specific grants.* Policy of this order – initiating general grants, the creation of the polytechnics, the creation of the Schools Council – could emanate from civil

*There are about three hundred Under-Secretaries in the Civil Service. They earn £6850 a year, and get into *Who's Who*.

servants, though only Ministers could accept, promote, modify or reject them. All were too important, too clearly political, for civil servants to do other than recommend and prepare the ground for them.

As Crosland says, an Under-Secretary put forward many of the fourteen points on teacher supply which he advocated ministerially. Under-Secretaries, and their subordinates, are thus policy makers, though in each of these examples nothing could have happened without ministerial sanctioning.* And any of them could, of course, have been started by Ministers. So no civil servant prompted Stewart and Crosland to 'go comprehensive', or Crosland to set up the Public Schools Commission or the National Council for Educational Technology.

This brings me to the role of the civil servant as perceived by Crosland and Boyle. In Mill's words, it is the Minister who receives 'the whole praise of what is well done, the whole blame of what is ill'.[28] But as Crosland points out, the system punishes incompetence harshly, and civil servants are simply not as anonymous as legend persistently relates (see p. 180). Civil servants' roles are far too often seen either as grossly dominant or as utterly subservient in terms of what they can do (the authority to use discretion and develop their role).

Most civil servants are like most Ministers – inadequate to fully exploit the potentialities of their role. But, in the view of this former administrator, the literature makes far too many concessions to Ministerial narcissism. The ability of even the most able Minister to create, promote and carry out policies is limited.

One senior civil servant at Education with whom I have discussed this point said that 'I can honestly say that there is not one new policy in my sector of responsibility that I have not either started or substantially contributed to over the last twenty years.'

It is inherently unlikely that a Minister can control all of

---

*I do not share Boyle's view that the Under-Secretary 'is the moment at which administration and policy meet', because policy making starts at any point where the limits of a policy are tested and changes are sought. This can be with a lively minded Assistant Principal, or higher executive officer (to use the pre-Fulton designations).

the activities, let alone generate all the policy initiatives, in a department such as the DES. Ministers come in with, as it were, a shopping list of intentions or goals. The civil servants analyse the advantages and the penalties of following one course rather than another (see Crosland on the Public Schools Commission, p. 184). But civil servants, too, present shopping lists to Ministers. It is they who construe the Ministerial value judgements about what society wants in terms of what local authorities and their institutions can provide and in terms of what resources central government can offer. Or if Ministers have no values to contribute, civil servants will. A policy objective might be decades in the making. 'Secondary education for all', for example, was a doctrine implicit in the Hadow reports of the 1930s but eventually brought into legislation in 1944. The making of policy is continuously in the hands of civil servants who create, as it were, low-frequency policy waves. Ministers bring in with them high-frequency activity which can initiate, change, strengthen or condemn a whole policy.

Ministers are, indeed, responsible for stating goals and objectives and for making sure that they are pursued. But as Boyle puts it, 'all of us imply values in whatever we say; that applies to civil servants too and it is no enlargement of their function, is no false attribution, to recognize that they will also have their own preferences' (p. 75). On returning to the Department as Minister in 1962 Boyle noticed how the Department had changed its stance on several issues. This was partly because 'new officials are coming to positions of authority and their value judgements are a factor in the situation as well'. He agreed that 'the assumption that there are predetermined and static suppositions within bureaucracy is nonsense' (p. 84).

The constraints on the Minister's role are not of authority or of civil service deviousness, but time and competence. To work out and work through a new pattern of educational development requires time and expertise.* Policy making de-

*In Sweden, for example, comprehensive schools were introduced after a long period of academic theorizing, and a controlled experiment in which schools in two areas of Stockholm were matched.

pends on assessments of existing services as against future needs. While to declare and sanction values is the role of the Minister, the detailed development of services in terms of those sanctioned values is unlikely to be achieved by politicians moved between the Board of Trade or the Treasury and the Department of Education every second year. And some would argue that in detailed development the true value-bases of objectives are also developed and changed. Crosland and Boyle are unusually gifted men. Crosland had honed himself for office in both economic and social service departments through his own writing and the painstaking thought that went behind it.

Few Ministers can or do prepare themselves in this way. When they don't, the Department will have its 'own' policies to continue and refine and prepare. There is also disjunction between the time scales of politics and of policy formation. Crosland says, 'I reckon it takes you six months to get your head properly above water, a year to get the general drift of most of the field, and two years really to master the whole of a Department.' He also argues that 'in your two years you can certainly lay down long-term objectives in the central fields ... though ... you will seldom see them finally achieved.' He argues that since the best talent is rare it ought to be mobile to give all Departments their share of it (p. 159). This may be so. But if so it does not enable the political entity anywhere to see objectives through, since the Cabinet and Prime Minister – which exist together more continuously than any individual Minister – do not scan and control the formation of objectives.*

Ministers have the authority to veto, to sanction or to promote policies for themselves or by instructing civil servants. They ensure that democratic values prevail by being available for Parliamentary scrutiny. Yet both Ministers are somewhat undaunted by the limitations that time prescribed. Boyle did not feel 'hustled' and was surprised when a civil servant assumed that he would want to take the impending 1964 General Election into account when making a decision. 'The only sensible line to take was to assume you had ... all the time in the

*Time will show whether the Capability Unit of a dozen or so outside experts will make this generalization obsolete.

world, that ... there was no crisis except for the next ball'
(p. 79). This would not be Crosland's view, but he, as well as
Boyle, was a bit nerveless about the fate of his most important
policy initiatives – comprehensives, public schools, educational priority areas, educational technology – once he moved
to work elsewhere. The value setters have to leave quite a lot
to the system, and to the Ministers who succeed them.

Role relationships are complex and the boundaries unclear.
The only plain differentiation barely describes the process at all –
Ministers alone can sanction a new or veto an existing policy.

As far as the *style* of the relationship is concerned, no feeling emerges that civil servants are obstructive. See how effectively Boyle and Crosland demolish the lessons drawn from
Dalton's account of Arthur Henderson's entry to the Foreign
Office in 1929[29] that the first twenty-four hours are conclusive
in determining relationships, as if Ministers were the Allies
creating the Normandy beachhead in 1944. Boyle happily
denies that there is a ju-jitsu contest between Ministers and
civil servants (p. 80). A few Ministers – Brown, Crossman and
Short, for example – have left Whitehall feeling that officials
cheated them of their purpose. Outsiders in for a while – as
anthologized recently by Hugh Thomas – not only attack the
amateur status of the administrative civil servant but also the
power of the administrator against the Minister.[30] Thomas
Balogh reckoned that 'the power of the headship of the
Treasury and Civil Service has grown to menace the future of
the country'. This authority is now divided and appointments
are recommended by a committee of Permanent Secretaries.

Ministers and Pressure Groups

Time limitations are one constraint. Pressure groups both
constrain and stimulate. The education service is not unique
in this respect but it works within a particularly strong and
long-lived professional constituency which might be called the
old educational establishment.

Thus, neither Crosland nor Boyle would have thought to
move very far without consulting Sir William Alexander, Secretary to the Association of Education Committees, Sir Ronald
Gould, Secretary to the National Union of Teachers, and their

counterparts in the other local authority and teachers' organizations (see pp. 134 and 175). Such officials as William Alexander constitute a powerful – perhaps the most powerful – entity within the education service for a far longer period than any Minister or Permanent Secretary and most senior officials within the Department. They know well the service for which they work and command trust and respect from those whom they represent. In the last resort, it is true, central government has its way. There is no sense of 'partnership' – no matter what the Department or Boyle says – when it comes to the larger decisions.* Thus, even on local government reorganization, an issue involving the whole future of those consulted, the government, acting perhaps on the advice of a Royal Commission, will make up its own mind, having received advice or remonstrance from the local authority associations. But they undoubtedly strongly influence Ministers' exercise of authority and the substance of their decisions. Thus Crosland's decision that local authorities should be 'requested' and not 'required' to go comprehensive was written in after discussions with the local authority associations. His decision that parents should be consulted about reorganization was the result of meeting with one of the new pressure groups, the Confederation for the Advancement of State Education. Consultation with teachers was written in after talks with the teacher associations.[31]

Boyle was asked where policies came from – from the Conservative Central Office, the Party Conference, Cabinet decisions, the Prime Minister, MPs, his own head?
He replied:

... this is the difference between education and some other subjects, I would say overwhelmingly the biggest number originated from ... the 'education world', if you like, from the logic of the education service as it was developing (p. 89).

Teacher supply policy he saw as created by the thinking of

---

*In writing to the local authority and teacher associations about the establishment of the Curriculum Study Group within the Ministry on 16 March 1962, the Permanent Secretary, Dame Mary Smieton, used the phrase 'our partners'. Partnership means shared accountability and authority, or nothing.

the NACST.* But he also attributed a lot, as did Crosland (see pp. 119 and 165), to the testing of policies with MPs. Boyle, indeed, goes further to imply that there is a bipartisan educational group in the House – a point Crosland refuted later in conversation with the author.

If local authority opinion is important, note one unexpected clue to traffic in the opposite direction which appears in the discussion with Edward Boyle (p. 122). Christopher Chataway† was appointed leader of the ILEA on the decision not only of the GLC leader, Desmond Plummer, but also the Chairman of the national Party – Edward du Cann – and the Chief Whip to the Parliamentary Party – William Whitelaw.‡ This could never happen in the Labour Party, or other than in London.

During the 1960s a new educational Establishment also developed. From Eccles's administration onwards, both educational journalism and the Ministry's own Information Division grew in strength. Such writers as Stuart Maclure, Tyrrell Burgess, Anne Corbett and Brian MacArthur are read and taken seriously by policy makers. The journalists were part of a wider network that grew in the 1950s and 1960s. The impact of the sociologists – Floud, Halsey, Michael Young – and the economists, led by John Vaizey, has already been mentioned. And social scientists have become far more numerous and powerful in the last decade. Economists have always been employed in the Treasury. Other Departments, including the DES, now have them on the staff. And such journals as *New Society* (founded in 1961) nourish both the general and scholarly interest in education as a subject. Before Vaizey published *The Costs of Education* in 1955 hardly a single academic paid attention to education. There is also now an articulate group of practitioner-advocates who keep up pressure for change within the system and in the Department: Alec Clegg, Margaret Miles, Harry Rée, and many others who have joined the better established 'official spokesmen' of the service. The NUS has

*The National Advisory Council on the Supply and Training of Teachers. Though appointed by the Minister its membership was a veritable roll call of the old Establishment.

†Joint Parliamentary Under-Secretary for Education 1962–4. Minister of Posts and Telecommunications since June 1970.

‡Leader of the House of Commons since June 1970.

leaders who negotiate with Ministers and Vice-Chancellors and have ready access to the mass media. These networks are almost wholly expansionist and radical, although there is now also an 'anti-intelligentsia' which publishes black papers.

All of this created, as Boyle agrees, 'a climate of opinion that ten years later a radical conservative, such as yourself [Boyle] was able to confirm as policy' (see p. 92). And the Ministry moved with the climate of opinion. A decision by Sir David Eccles did most perhaps, to open up education to a wider constituency. His appointment of an economist, Geoffrey Crowther, as Chairman to the Central Advisory Council for Education brought in a distinguished outsider to examine and help sponsor a major section of the service.* From then on, it became a commonplace. The Robbins Committee had, too, a sophisticated secretariat helped by a research team led by Claus Moser, the first of the social science professors to be brought into full-time, if temporary, work for the education service.† By the time the study of primary education came to be established it was still novel, but not astonishing, that Boyle appointed the Wykeham Professor of Logic at Oxford, an LSE professor and one of the world's leading child development experts as members.‡ Their expertise, and opinions based on their own professional and personal commitments, interacted with those presented to the Committee by the educational world.

A further network was personal to Crosland – an informal consultative group which met at his home in London (see p. 185). He was also active in bringing in social scientists, as paid advisors to the DES (p. 185).

It is difficult to think of a similar congregation of outsiders

*Geoffrey Crowther is Chairman of several major official committees and latterly of the Commission on the Constitution. He was Chairman of the Central Advisory Council for Education 1956–60 which produced *15 to 18* – see p. 60, n. 13.

†Claus Moser is Professor of Social Statistics, London School of Economics, and seconded to Cabinet Office as Director, Central Statistical Office since 1967. He was statistical adviser to the Robbins Committee.

‡A. J. (now Sir Alfred) Ayer; Professor D. V. Donnison, Director of the Centre for Environmental Studies, Chairman of Public Schools Commission, formerly Professor of Social Administration, London School of Economics; and J. M. Tanner, Professor of Child Health and Growth, London University Institute of Child Health.

in other services who so influence and articulate the discussion of policy as in education.

The Impact of the Politician on Policies

Both Ministers presided over important realignments of policies. But what impact did they have individually? Since no Minister can adequately scan, let alone control, more than a small proportion of the policies for which he is accountable, it is government by exception. Most activities continue without Ministerial scrutiny and Ministers select for attention those which make special demands on resources or have a sharp political impact or a particularly strong ideological appeal. But a Minister should, Crosland says,

be constantly pushing and prodding and asking why things haven't been done. . . . An active Minister will himself initiate changes in policy; while even a passive Minister exercises a final right of veto (see p. 179).

Neither he nor Boyle expected to control everything and neither worried too much about it. Crosland puts it nicely:

. . . even after two years at the Board of Trade I had had no contact at all with the Patent Office and practically none with Weights and Measures. But I never lay awake at night thinking 'Gosh, I wonder what those chaps at the Patent Office are up to' (p. 179).

Later he emphasized:

A large part of any Department's work, which does not at that moment raise acute controversial issues, will go on without the Minister being involved at all . . . when I was Minister, I selected what seemed to me to be the crucial issues (p. 199).

In both Boyle and Crosland's time such questions as the education of the handicapped (except for pupils' allowances), large zones of further education policy, and teachers' pensions did not come sufficiently under their view for them to have had personal impact on them.

Ministers are subject to the constraints of the system already discussed. Crosland lists particularly the legacy of history – a vast and inert inheritance of outmoded buildings; the dispersal of decision making through a large number of bodies outside government control; the effectiveness of the pressure groups; and the financial constraints faced by the government of the day (p. 159). What, then, *can* Ministers do?

The precise roles of Ministers will remain obscure until papers are opened up and the interplay between the Ministers and other participants and in the process is made plain. We cannot now know with any certainty how Anthony Crosland and Edward Boyle affected the main policies with which they are publicly associated. With these reservations, take Anthony Crosland's most important decision – the issue of *Circular 10/65* which 'requested' local education authorities to submit plans for the reorganization of secondary education. Here Crosland inherited a draft of the circular from Michael Stewart,* had a clear mandate from his party, and used it.†

But his own role was important. First it was a key test of relationships between the centre and local authorities – particularly important in view of the suspicion in which some parts of the service initially held him.‡ He was known to be a determined politician and it would have surprised no one had

*Michael Stewart was Secretary of State for Education and Science, October 1964–January 1965, before going to the Foreign Office and D E A.

†Boyle's belief (p. 78) that reorganization was already largely under way does not diminish the importance of *Circular 10/65*. Otherwise Mrs Thatcher (Secretary of State for Education and Science from June 1970) would hardly have bothered to change the policy in her *Circular 10/70*.

‡His arrival at Curzon Street was welcomed by officials, many of whom could hardly believe the way in which Michael Stewart, so cogent and well informed in opposition, had chosen to cloister himself with his papers.

His reputation as a rigorous thinker and an able Minister at the Department of Economic Affairs had preceded him. The wider educational world watched him more warily. *Education*, a journal which can, at times, combine considerable nastiness with ineffable dreariness, on 29 January 1965 said: 'With the arrival of Mr Anthony Crosland, the Department of Education and Science has exchanged the solid, professional, middle-of-the-road qualities of Mr Stewart for a less predictable, more brilliant, more controversial personality.' He was 'highly intelligent and has the reputation of a wicked conversationalist with a gift for amusing and malicious disputation. He is accused by his enemies – of whom, within the Labour Party, he seems to have unlimited number – of being merciless at tearing his opponents to shreds while himself being thin skinned and easily offended.' And, 'he is impatient and intolerant, a man of words, who must find the slow and laborious business of negotiation and consultation tiresome and tedious.' In my judgement *Education* showed little knowledge of either Stewart or Crosland, as its own summaries of Crosland's achievements in 1967 showed very clearly. Both *Education* and *The Times Educational Supplement* wrote in glowing terms of his two years of progress.

he decided to use legal compulsion. That this was explicitly a matter of political, Ministerial judgement is plain from the fact that his own Minister of State, Reg Prentice,* and some of his back-benchers, disagreed with his decision to 'request' rather than 'require' local education authorities to submit schemes (see p. 189). So, at this time, no legal compulsion was used, though Crosland was determined to get action quickly and a special team to implement the policy was set up in the DES. The decision to be non-prescriptive in style was his to make. Edward Short reached the point of seeking legal authority to prescribe towards the end of his administration (when the local government elections had swept Labour councils out of office), only to be frustrated by inefficient whipping† and loss of office. Secondly, as we will see (p. 190) Crosland decided to include consultation with parents and teachers. Thirdly, though this does not emerge from the interview, Crosland must have decided that he could achieve what one might regard as one of the most important Socialist actions of the Labour government without much more resources than the extra building committed for raising the school-leaving age. He allowed for wide variations in organizational patterns and gave detailed guidance to that effect. He decided that experiment in patterns and, with it, some deference to local opinion would be beneficial. Ministers could have, at a high cost, chosen to be far more prescriptive. The Swedes, for example, founded a ten-year programme for changing to a comprehensive system which makes a more radical reorganization of what is admittedly a far smaller and less complicated system. Crosland decided to go ahead with his revolutionary proposal and get action – local authority schemes – within one year. But the style was collaborative, experimental, even cautious. The technical advice on how it might be achieved came from HMIs (p. 188) and administrators. He made the major

*Reginald Prentice was a Minister of State of the DES, October 1964–January 1967, when he became Minister for Overseas Development.

†Not to be confused with his support for the teachers' professional right to decide whether children should be beaten with canes or tawses. Edward Short (Secretary of State for Education and Science, April 1968–June 1970) lost his bill enforcing comprehensive schooling because the government failed to have a majority of members present for the critical division.

decisions and set the pace and style. He deliberately set out to win confidence and displayed the bureaucratic virtue of action *studio et sine ira.* Local authorities got to know they could rely on him to negotiate and not to push policies down their throats. Had he sought a change of law there might have been a major political row attracting public support to the comprehensive issue and a faster programme which would have made it marginally more difficult for Mrs Thatcher to reverse his policy within three days of gaining office. His own view was that local authorities and the Department could not have created change more quickly even with legal power behind them (p. 191).

Crosland took other major decisions: he established the Public Schools Commission, the National Council for Educational Technology and the Department's own Planning Branch. The Public Schools Commission embraced his own political philosophy.* The relative failure of these three moves displays

*He wrote: 'The public schools offend not only against "the weak", let alone "the strong" ideal of equal opportunity; they offend even more against any ideal of social cohesion or democracy. This privileged stratum of education, the exclusive preserve of the wealthier classes, socially and physically segregated from the state educational system, is the greatest single cause of stratification and class consciousness in Britain.... Small wonder the school system is the greatest divisive influence. It is no accident that Britain, the only advanced country with a national private elite system of education, should also be the most class-ridden country.... We must then grasp the nettle of the public school, bearing in mind our basic objectives. These are threefold: firstly, to assimilate them into the state sector, so that they play a full and cooperative part in the national educational effort; secondly, to democratize their entry and so destroy their present socially exclusive character; thirdly, to create a more genuine equality of opportunity by limiting the power of the rich to buy social privilege through buying private education.... You must either have a radical reform or none at all and we might ... get the desired social mixture by the operation of free choice. But if we do not and the demand remains heavily slanted, the authorities must deliberately allocate free places in proportion either to certain broadly defined income brackets or to different types of state schools.... A Labour government must give high priority to this reform.... If a majority of the schools refuse to accept a voluntary reform, then the community must assert the right to legislate.' Here, in *The Conservative Enemy* (1962), is the origin of the Public Schools Commission, established under the chairmanship of Sir John Newsom in December 1965 'to advise on the best way of integrating the public schools with the state system of

how a Minister is dependent upon a helpful economic environment and a strong collective will. But in each case he, and he
alone, took the initiative. Civil servants cautioned (p. 183),
advised, and then got on with implementing the Minister's
decisions.

Other policies of Crosland demonstrate that Ministers in-
herit policies which they can accept or reject. Crosland was
troubled with uncertainty about the proposal to create two
parallel systems of higher education (the 'binary' system) and
he criticizes civil servants for forcing a decision too early on
him (p. 193). The decision to create thirty polytechnics was not
at all in line with the Labour Party's Taylor Committee recommendations of a few years earlier to create a large and un-
differentiated system of higher education.* It must have been
created by the Department responding to local authority wishes.

But Crosland could have deferred or reversed the decision.
After all, within a few days of reaching the Board of Trade he
reversed Douglas Jay's decision that the Stansted site should
be used for the third London Airport. And Mrs Thatcher's
reversal of *Circular 10/65* (in *Circular 10/70* signed by the
same Permanent Secretary, Herbert Andrew†) shows that
Ministers can reverse policies drastically and quickly.

Many decisions which Crosland took, including those to
leave established policies alone, and the weight he placed behind them, reflected his political values; even the decision to
create the Council for Educational Technology echoed the 1964
government's enthusiasm for technology. Other policies
neither Boyle nor Crosland originated. There would have been
growth in educational investment whatever the party or per-

---

education'. Its first report appeared in July 1968, after which Professor
David Donnison became the Commission's Chairman. The second report
appeared in 1970.

*The Labour Party Study Group on Higher Education, whose report *The
Years of Crisis* was published in 1963. Crosland was a member.

†This demonstrates the acceptance by civil servants of the principle that
they must be available to implement Ministers' policies even when this
involves them in quite strong changes in direction. It does not imply that
Andrew gave contradictory advice. Sir (George) Herbert Andrew was Permanent Under-Secretary of State for Education and Science, 1964–70. He
was previously Second Secretary to the Board of Trade.

son of the Minister. Crosland's 'fourteen points' (noted on pp. 191–2) for the supply and deployment of teachers contained little that was new – some of them, in fact, were known in the Department after the civil servant who invented many of them a few years before. But Crosland kicked them into life and decided to brave NUT and other opposition to them. He says he would have done the same with the proposals in the *Plowden Report* had he stayed longer at Education (p. 197). He made a start by winning £16 million for the educational priority areas.

Crosland thus selected his own field of battle. He need not but did defend his service – the raising of the school-leaving age was safe with him but not with his successor Patrick Gordon Walker. He affected the environment if not the structure of educational government by deciding not to reappoint the English and Welsh Central Advisory Councils and the National Advisory Council for the Training and Supply of Teachers. Boyle took a different view of them, and would have done otherwise (p. 132).

The contrast with Boyle is important. The Conservative equivalent to Crosland was Eccles rather than Boyle. Both Eccles and Crosland had views which they pressed hard in terms of actual policies. Boyle was somewhat less of an originator, coming earlier to the scene, and changed the ethos, level and style of discourse within which policies were made. Thus the main events of his Ministry (pp. 66–8) show many decisions for which he was responsible but which emanated from an education service already expanding fast under its own momentum, or from the Department's, rather than the Minister. To explain his role adequately, I must treat his career in a little more detail than Crosland's, if only because clear changes of direction are more difficult to discern.

First, he came as a young junior Minister destined to reach the top but who had voluntarily resigned on an issue of principle.*

This inner toughness is belied by his gentleness of manner,

---

*Churchill had made him, at thirty-one, Parliamentary Secretary to the Ministry of Supply. He was appointed Economic Secretary to the Treasury in 1955 by Anthony Eden until, with Eden's Suez adventure, he was moved to

which was exploited in a telling if cheap metaphor by Henry
Fairlie, who wrote: 'Sir Edward is one of the few politicians
today who ... suggests that if one sticks one's finger into him
one will eventually strike something hard.'[32] His resignation
over Suez came at a time when the Tory party in the country
wanted more rather than less drastic action. He could have
easily been relegated to the obscurity of one who resigns at
the wrong time. It provided critical mass to the landslide
that was soon to overtake Eden and his policy. Later, when
again under attack for his educational liberalism, he was
one of twenty-five Conservative MPs who abstained from
voting on the second reading of the 1968 Race Relations Bill.

These political attitudes are part of his intellectual and
emotional make-up. He believes in an open society and re-
serves his contempt for the worthlessly privileged and the
intolerant. And these attitudes, more than specific policies,
were what he contributed at Minister, and what no one else
in the education world at that time could have contributed
with such weight. His role was primarily one of charisma.
This was evident in his first days as Parliamentary Secretary.
I was Boyle's Private Secretary from January 1956 to October
1958 and met him for the first time with a group of determined television men at the steps of Curzon Street House on
the Friday evening of his return to government.

The appointment had come over the tapes on a release from
Number Ten although the Minister of Education, according
to the Education Act of 1944 (Section 1), appoints his own
Parliamentary Secretary. This provision is idiosyncratic to
the law of education. Once appointed, the junior Minister dis-
appears from statutory and, if he is not careful, from all other
view as well. He has no legal functions: only an office, a private secretary and a collection of black and red boxes. 'There
are few Departments where any normally intelligent Parliamentarian couldn't do the junior job all right ...' as Boyle
puts it (p. 86). And Crosland makes it plain that junior Ministers cannot take a major decision by themselves and that delega-

---

resign in November 1956 because, in the terms of his letter to the Prime
Minister, 'I do not honestly feel that I can defend, as a Minister, the recent
policy of the government.'

tion to them of minor matters varies, according to their ability (p. 157). This underlines the cruelty of the system – get to the very top or be nothing.

It was what Boyle found. He was too quick for the load placed on him and soon ran out of cases. The issues delegated him were resolutions of opposed compulsory purchase orders, the closure of village schools, the disqualification of teachers reported for unprofessional behaviour (usually different varieties of buggery or burglary), special services (the education of the handicapped, the school medical services, the school meal and milk services) and a stream of Parliamentary questions, adjournment debates, committee stage defence of the 1958 Local Government Bill,* and other miscellaneous Parliamentary business. When, however, Hailsham became Minister, but had not yet reverted to the common state, Boyle took all of the Department's business in the House of Commons.† This kept him more fully occupied.‡ The contrast between Education and the Treasury was, however, great and this led him to consider his role as a Minister in a social service Department, where there is simply not as much 'political' business or direct decision making by Ministers as at, say, the Home or Foreign Offices.

At that time Viscount Templewood's autobiography had just been published. Hoare, as he then was, found himself Secretary of State for Air in 1924, when the Air Force had little social status or public support. Hoare made it his business to ensure that the career of an Air Force pilot became as acceptable to the upper middle classes as a career in a good county regiment.**

---

*No mean task this. It incorporated the substitution of specific by general grants and was politically hard going as well as exceedingly technical.

†In June 1970, Quintin Hogg again assumed the peerage so as to be able to sit on the Woolsack.

‡Once, for example, he had to answer debates four times in three days in the House. On the fourth occasion he promised the Speaker that 'this is positively my last appearance this week'.

**This point, and the analogy with the present status of maintained schools, was made in a review of Templewood's *Empire of the Air* (Collins, 1957) by Michael Howard in the *New Statesman*, 26 January 1957. He

With this analogy in mind, Boyle decided to use his enormous gifts to enhance the status of the maintained school system and convert the large and ignorant middle area of public opinion to its support. And so he visited most, if not all, the 146 local education authorities in two and a half years.* He not only made contact with remote places, but brought style and the statement of liberal views to them. He was a gifted, gracious and informal guest.† He would quickly get off ritual pronouncement and on to personal statements about what he saw in the schools and how they reflected the increasing potential good of our society. He would maintain that education produced the opportunities that we all wanted, that if it meant more people owning cars and driving them to places

---

wrote: 'The basic reason why our state educational system, on paper one of the finest in the world, has failed to create equality of opportunity is that no Minister of Education has ever really attempted to win for it, in realistic social terms, parity of esteem. It was not enough, in this absurd country, to make state schools efficient; they should also have been made smart in the way in which the Hoares set out to make the Air Force smart.' This review struck a chord in Boyle.

*All Ministers visit a lot of local authorities; Boyle did more than most.

†He was kind to the most inept of hosts. And some were very inept: he was introduced at one prize-giving in these terms: 'I now have pleasure in introducing Sir Edwin Boyle, B.T., who is Secretary to the Treasurer.' He was also occasionally absent minded – he could pick up a copy of the *Guardian* at a reception in a Mayor's parlour while his hosts waited to chat with him. And 'If that is shaving soap on his face, should he not get it off before he is photographed?' one tough Alderman asked.

Boyle could be relatively negligent of convention. He stretched the rules of the Carlton Club – which allows only those eligible to be elected to be invited as guests – by inviting, with the permission of the Chairman, civil servants. This must have irritated colleagues who seemed peeved to find him dining with a Private Secretary and thus unavailable for gossip on the night when three Treasury Ministers – Thorneycroft, Powell and Birch – resigned in protest against the lack of support given them by the Cabinet in restraining government expenditure. Boyle, in fact, became Financial Secretary to the Treasury after this exodus of the high minded.

As a Minister, he was generous of time, and indeed of everything else. Good bottles used to emanate from him to a massive network of former Private Secretaries and other associates at Christmas time. When I once admitted to him, during a railway journey, that I had read no Jane Austen, he evaded an official reception party to dive into a bookshop to buy a complete set.

that they would not otherwise see, this was all the better for them and for the rest of us. Like Crosland, he has no great patience with preservation for its own sake.[33]

When on 13 July 1962 Harold Macmillan dismissed seven Ministers from office, including David Eccles, Boyle returned from the Treasury to become, at thirty-nine, the youngest Minister of Education and the youngest member of the Cabinet.

He began with many advantages. He had served in two of the most prestigious junior Minister posts – Economic and later Financial Secretary to the Treasury. He had served in his Department as a successful junior Minister. He had got to know the main pressure groups and senior civil servants with whom he would have to work, and they liked him. So far from damaging his career, his resignation at the time of the Suez adventure had served to place him high in the opinions of those who mattered. Comparisons with the young Churchill – articulate and imaginative but unafraid to dissent, even at the cost of office, but getting away with it as well – were beginning to be made.

Given these advantages, what did Boyle do that was distinctively his? On some issues he took a firm line or made a strong contribution – the expansion of teacher supply, the timing of raising the school-leaving age, the unfreezing of legal restrictions on the creation of middle schools, the government's new role in salary negotiations. He made comprehensive and non-streamed schools discussable even if not acceptable to his party. He believed in curriculum development and the eradication of the baleful effect of external examinations on it. While he identified these as government policies his main contribution was to bring style and influence to the education service. If, as one observer* put it, Boyle was

* 'So far as the establishment is concerned he is the complete "insider" whose grandfather, the first Baronet, was a Conservative MP. After Eton, he became President of the Union of Oxford and entered Parliament in 1950. As an "insider" he knows how to work on the inside for what is important to the Establishment. And for him the important thing is that the establishment should look forward, not back.' Andrew Routh, *Education*, 20 July 1962.
But how does one boundary define the 'insider' or the Establishment

the complete insider (but see how Boyle refutes the obvious stereotype of him as the Etonian heir to an Etonian line) he used his position from within the party to advance the claims of an expanding maintained system to the middle-class voter and to his own party. So, in discussing Professor Bantock's statement, 'Anyone of real ability can now make the grade, if that is the word for it',[34] Boyle says,

... the norm of opinion by 1965 was clearly on Robbins side and not on Bantock's ... if I contributed anything to education ... I did something to bring 'middle opinion' over to this side, to make it plain that the norm of opinion had shifted ... (p. 92).

And again, on his famous preface to the *Newsom Report*:

It was somebody else's doctrine, but I alone, at that moment, was in a position to give official blessing to it (p. 94).

Again, however, there is a difference between Boyle and Crosland. Crosland propounded new policies, some of which failed. Boyle did not establish explicit policies that would enable all children to 'acquire their intelligence' – there was no equivalent of Crosland's sponsoring of educational priority areas.

The differences between Crosland's and Boyle's impact derive partly from personal preferences and style, partly from the political values they carried with them, and partly from circumstances. While Boyle did not find it hard to fight for educational expansion, Crosland advanced new policies which made him an active Minister. Crosland tried to do more and failed to achieve some of his largest ambitions. This was not lack of authority in his role but lack of time and, to some extent at least, of resources, for the two radical moves dearest to his heart – the eradication of public and selective schools. He could not do for education what Bevan did for the health service – bring the proud teaching hospitals into a state system.

---

which he is inside? In fact, Boyle preferred the company not of the baronets of his own party but the younger academics and administrators with whom he could talk politics, history, philosophy and music. His grandfather was a Liberal and not a Conservative MP.

Crosland was rare in his time in pressing for the establishment of a Planning Branch which would identify his Department's objectives. Since his time as Secretary of State, the *Fulton Reoprt* and its aftermath have advanced the claims of management by objectives, and the Heath government has begun its programme analysis review in the DES, as elsewhere, so that the Capability Unit can collate policy options for collective government decision. Both he and Boyle were rare in their time in articulating objectives; they are now slightly dated by the rush of management systems thinking that is said to be starting to permeate the civil service.[35] Crosland maintains the need, however, not to be swept overboard by these changes and, indeed, argues for a separate social service study unit (see pp. 32 and 163).[36]

These developments may change Ministerial roles. Rational process drives out the prophetic and the evangelical. Ministers will be less able to fly by the seats of their pants if systems thinking takes over. The ablest will, however, be capable of doing more than could Boyle and Crosland because options will be better identified and costed. This is surely the lesson to be learned from Robert MacNamara's career at the US Department of Defense. Lesser Ministers will find their discretion even more tightly squeezed.

Edward Boyle and Anthony Crosland were two of the Ministers most able to state and implement their policies. In differing degrees, they had mandates for change, and where they had no mandate they created it by clear statement and force of personality. Inasmuch as their achievements were limited, they help demarcate the limits of Ministerial action within the education service as it is now administered. What they could not achieve, few others could achieve either.

Notes

1. C. B. Cox and A. E. Dyson (eds.), *Black Paper One (Fight for Education)*, *Black Paper Two (The Crisis in Education)*, Critical Quarterly Society, 1969, 1970.

2. S. E. Finer, 'The individual responsibility of Ministers', *Public Administration*, vol. 34, Winter 1956. The same point is made by A. H. Birch, *Representative and Responsible Government*, Allen & Unwin, 1964; and Geoffrey Marshall, 'Ministerial responsibility', *Political Quarterly*, vol. 34, 1963.

3. Quoted by Anne Corbett, 'The Tory educators', *New Society*, 22 May 1969.

4. Interview with the *Birmingham Post*, 1959. Quoted by Andrew Routh, *Education*, 20 July 1962.

5. Central Advisory Council for Education (England), *Half Our Future (Newsom Report)*, H M S O, 1963.

6. Anne Corbett, 'The Tory educators'.

7. Central Advisory Council for Education (England), *Children and their Primary Schools (Plowden Report)*, H M S O, 1967, ch. 5.

8. *Sunday Times*, 26 February 1961.

9. *Daily Telegraph*, 20 October 1969.

10. Crosland's socialism is described in *The Future of Socialism*, Cape, 1956; *The Conservative Enemy*, Cape, 1962; and *A Social Democratic Britain*, Fabian Pamphlet, no. 404, 1971.

11. A. H. Halsey, 'The public schools debate', *New Society*, 25 June 1968.

12. David Eccles, *White Paper on Technical Education*, H M S O Cmd. 9703, 1956.

13. Central Advisory Council for Education (England), *15 to 18 (Crowther Report)*, H M S O, 1959, vol. 1, ch. 6.

14. *Plowden Report*, ch. 31.

15. *Report of the Consultative Committee on the Primary School (Hadow Report)*, H M S O, 1931, p. xxviii. R. H. Tawney, *Equality*, Allen & Unwin, 1931.

16. 'Compared with 216,000 students in full-time higher education in Great Britain in 1962–3, places should be available for about 390,000 in 1973–4, and, on present estimates, for about 560,000 in 1980–81.' *Report of the Committee appointed by the Prime Minister under the Chairmanship of Lord Robbins, 1961–3: Higher Education*, H M S O,

Cmnd. 2154, 1963, para. 17. But see Richard Layard, John King and Claus Moser, *The Impact of Robbins*, Penguin, 1969.

17. D. V. Donnison, 'Education and opinion', *New Society*, 26 October 1967. The first of these figures is close to those in the Plowden Report (1964) Survey of Parental Attitudes (vol. 2, Appendix 3, p. 110).

18. Central Advisory Council for Education (England), *Early Leaving*, HMSO, 1954. For Robbins, see particularly vol. 2, Pts II and III. J. W. B. Douglas, *Home and School*, MacGibbon & Kee, 1964.

19. J. Floud, A. H. Halsey and F. M. Martin, *Social Class and Educational Opportunity*, Heinemann, 1956.

20. Basil Bernstein, 'Social class and linguistic development', in A. H. Halsey (ed.), *Education, Economy and Society*, Free Press, 1961.

21. *Report of the Royal Commission on Local Government in London (Herbert Report)*, HMSO, Cmnd. 1164, 1960. *Report of the Royal Commission on Local Government in England (Maud Report) 1966–69*, HMSO, Cmnd. 4040, 1969.

22. *The Reorganization of Central Government*, HMSO, Cmnd. 4506, November 1970.

23. See, for example, J. A. C. Griffith, *Central Departments and Local Authorities*, Allen & Unwin, 1966.

24. For example, Ivor Jennings in *Cabinet Government* (Oxford University Press, 1959) stated: 'The Cabinet is the core of the British constitutional system .... It is the supreme directing authority.' And J. F. M. Macintosh, in *The British Cabinet* (Hutchinson, 1968): 'By the 1950s, the Cabinet dominated British government ...' On another point, P. Gordon Walker in *The Cabinet* (Cape, 1969): 'All Ministers are really equals; all are expected to state their views with the utmost frankness.' Both Clement Attlee and Harold Wilson (in their interviews with Francis Williams and Norman Hunt, reproduced in A. King, *The Prime Minister* (Macmillan, 1969)) were more ambivalent – both talked of equality but gave strong examples to the contrary. R. H. S. Crossman, in his Introduction to Bagehot's *The English Constitution* (Collins, 1968), states boldly: 'We have Prime Ministerial government'. Macmillan's memoirs leave no doubt about who manages the country. No sooner had Macmillan kissed hands than he was at work appointing, dismissing and transferring Ministers, and stating the main immediate objectives of his administration (*Riding the Storm*, Macmillan, 1971).

25. *Report of the Machinery of Government Committee of the Ministry of Reconstruction, 1918 (Haldane Report)*, HMSO, Cd. 9230, 1918.

26. The Treasury used to be called the 'central organ of government' in Civil Service Commission literature. See also W. J. M. Mackenzie and J. W. Grove, *Central Administration in Britain*, Longman, 1957; and D. N. Chester and F. M. G. Willson, *The Organization of British Central Government 1910–1950*, Allen & Unwin, 1957.

27. See M. Kogan, 'Social services: their Whitehall status', *New Society*, 21 August 1969.

28. J. S. Mill, *Considerations on Representative Government*, ed. R. B. McCallum, Oxford University Press, 1946.

29. Hugh Dalton, *Call Back Yesterday: Memoirs 1887–1931*, Frederick Muller, 1953.

30. H. Thomas (ed.), *Crisis in the Civil Service*, Great Society Series, 1968. Some of the assumptions in this anthology are lopsided. For example, Dudley Seers states that understandings are usually reached without great difficulty ('I think I can persuade my Minister . . .') and these in turn provide officials with a valuable additional weapon when they need it ('I am sorry, Minister, but I know the Treasury would object to . . .'). Or, 'Civil servants naturally acquire after a time fairly definite views on what should be their Department's policy. Some of the ideas of the incoming Minister will probably seem to the Permanent Secretary not merely without precedent but wildly impracticable, or even obviously contrary to the national interest. They might involve the Department in a lot more work or in activities of a kind that would expose it to attacks in the press. This is bound to affect not merely the Permanent Secretary's advice, but the way in which he puts it forward – how thoroughly alternative policies are explained and how much information from which wrong conclusions might be drawn is provided.' None of the three Permanent Secretaries under whom I served gave a moment's thought to the amount of work a Minister's demands might create. I simply do not recall any case in which advice was loaded in the way Seers suggests. If they thought a policy bad or mad they were more likely to say so than obscure the facts or the arguments.

31. All of these decisions were incorporated in the famous *Circular 10/65* which was issued on 12 July 1965 and 'called attention to the government's declared objective to end selection at 11-plus and eliminate separation in secondary education', gave detailed guidance on possible interim as well as long-term methods of achieving this objective, and requested local education authorities to submit plans for their areas within a year. See DES, *Education in 1965, being the Report of the Department of Education and Science*, HMSO, Cmnd. 2938, 1965.

to give away an extra £250 million in tax reliefs.
periment did not succeed. There was a decline in
and a balance of payments deficit of nearly £800
ich Maudling tackled through an International
Fund credit by obtaining a Statement of Intent on
incomes restraint from the TUC which did not,
ened, materialize.
ming up the economic climate during this period w
e with Brittan that it was an interesting 'unfinished
nt', characterized by large hopes and some
y gains collapsing eventually into deficit. Perhaps,
ts most remarkable feature was the buoyancy whic
ver most of 1962 and 1963 and part of 1964.
e difficulties confronted by the Chancellor, the
ducation was able to benefit from general policie
s Boyle's successes in sustaining growth –
igher education – indicate.

f Boyle's periods of office as Minister were:

ed 'a major inquiry by the National
cational Research into the effects of
schools'.

Education's Curriculum Study Group.

cil on the Training and Supply of
rt on the Demand and Supply of
he Future Pattern of Education and

ion on teacher-training building,

awards to students.

£1000 million for the first

employers and teachers
£21 million salary
g from Parliament a

32. Henry Fairlie, 'On resignation: the battlefield or the playground of conscience', *National and English Review*, vol. 148, April 1967, p. 186.

33. See A. Crosland, *A Social Democratic Britain*, particularly section 5, 'False trails'.

34. S. H. Bantock, *Education and Values*, Faber, 1965.

35. C. H. Sisson, 'Civil service reform', *Spectator*, 21 and 28 February and 6 March 1971, provides a serving civil servant's reaction to these attempts.

36. This is one lesson to be drawn from the US Office of Education's fate under the controls of the Bureau of the Budget and other external evaluation systems. See the Report of the OECD examiners in *Research and Development in Education in the USA*, OECD, Paris, 1971.

Edward Boyle

Interviewed on 4 and 5 December 1970 at
the Vice-Chancellor's Lodge, University of Leeds

Parliamentary Secretary to the Ministry of Educati
January 1957 to October 1959, Minister of Educa
July 1962 to April 1964, and Minister of State fo
(responsible for higher education), with a seat
until 16 October 1964.

Introduction

As ever, the period was dominated by
Reginald Maudling took over the Treas
Lloyd on 13 July 1962 he was determ
growth. But the economy's underlyin
reflected in the balance of paymen
a small surplus of £14 million in 19
1964 of £35 and £747 million res
at $2·80 was an enormous strain
decline in the competitiveness
of world markets was falling
and the erosion of her gold a

Despite the underlying p962
during the period, Mau n-tu
and his policies show a new
was to relax purchase . The
Samuel Brittan's phr
Maudling respond
capital expenditu f
attempt to enc in
nurtured by Nm
Faster Gro St
growth ra
Market
1963.

*Much
The Role of t

Reconstituted English and Welsh Central Advisory Councils for Education to 'consider primary education in all its aspects and the transition from primary to secondary education'. These became the Plowden and Gittins Committees (which reported in 1967).

Increased Ministry research fund from £20,000 to £70,000 in 1963–4.

Encouraged experiments in organization of secondary education. Said in a speech to the Annual Conference of Association of Education Committees: 'We do no longer regard any pattern of organization as the "norm" compared with which all others must be stigmatized.'

Announced greatly increased school-building programmes for 1965–6 and 1966–7, including £25–30 million set aside for primary and secondary improvements.

Welcomed recommendations of Robbins Report 'as an opportunity to set the course of higher education in this country for a generation'. Said: 'Courses of higher education should be available for all of those who are qualified by ability and attainment to pursue them.' Accepted Robbins costing and planning, and negotiations for its implementation began right away.

Act passed to create middle schools by cutting across existing definitions of primary and secondary education.

Published Report of Newsom Committee, *Half Our Future*.

1964 Announced: 'It is the government's intention that the school-leaving age should be raised to sixteen in 1970–71.'

Principal Medical Officer to the Ministry, Peter Henderson, made a speech suggesting that pre-marital sexual experience should not be condemned. Boyle's defence of his right to make speech led to attacks on him for endorsing the 'new morality'.

Sanctioned the creation of the Schools Council for the Curriculum and Examinations, to replace the Secondary School Examinations Council.

On 20 March Edward Boyle announced the creation of the new Department of Education and Science, to consist of 'four administrative units, one of which will deal with universities and civil science, and the others with schools and other education in England and Wales'. Two Ministers of State (one to be Boyle) were to serve the new Secretary of State (Quintin Hogg).

Boyle retained his seat in the Cabinet until the Labour General Election victory in October 1964. He was last seen in the Department as a Minister as the television on the fourth floor of Curzon Street House, where Ministers have their offices, was showing Harold Wilson securing his majority of six seats in the House of Commons. Boyle walked out after a few graceful farewells. Hailsham came along soon afterwards, swinging his red box, and crying to no one in particular, 'Well, here we go again.'

Edward Boyle

The Attraction of Politics

You entered Parliament at the age of twenty-seven and within four years had become a junior Minister – Parliamentary Secretary to the Ministry of Supply. What made you enter politics?

I think I was first conscious of wanting to enter politics in 1943 at the time of the discussions on the *Beveridge Report*. Later, the discussions on the Employment White Paper of 1944, the controversies on economic policy after 1945 – all those things made me want to be an MP. I didn't have very strong party political feelings at that time, though, equally, I didn't have much doubt as to the side I wanted to join. It was the interest of the subjects themselves and the feeling that I would like to take part in discussing them. The aspect of politics I shall miss most is no longer being able to take part in House of Commons debates. Also I felt, rightly, that going into the House of Commons would enable me to encounter, work with, and perhaps conflict with, some of the ablest people of our era.

Did you have a choice? Was there a time when you felt it could be one of two or three things?

I don't recall ever considering anything else very seriously. I wasn't at all certain how soon I would get into the House of Commons; I realized I might have to do some temporary job in the intervening time. In that respect I was lucky in having a degree of financial independence. I also knew I could do some journalism. I assumed, perhaps too readily, that if I really wanted to get into the House of Commons I would be able to do so.

When Home's government lost the 1964 election, you led the Opposition first on Home Office and then on education affairs for four and a half years. Had you remained in politics, you would surely have returned as a senior Cabinet Minister. What made you leave politics?

Well, two things. First, I was enormously attracted by the offer of being Vice-Chancellor of Leeds University. It was the pull of the job I was offered and not, in any sense, a push away from politics that influenced me here. Secondly, you mentioned just now that I might have been a senior Cabinet Minister – I think perhaps that needs more analysis. If I had thought I was going to be Prime Minister or Chancellor of the Exchequer, that would have been a different matter. I don't myself think that there was much prospect of my having one of the top three or four jobs. You can get so far in politics by enthusiasm and, if you like, by ability; above that it's very much a matter of your position in the party, your relationship to the total picture, your image at a given time, as well as your leader's view about the composition he requires. I am not blaming anybody for this. I left the House of Commons with no feelings of disappointment or frustration of any kind. Some people, I think, look back on their career in the Commons with a certain amount of regret. That doesn't apply to me and I think I found it all the easier to leave it for that reason. Just as people who've got a happy home background find it easier to go away from home, so the fact that I look back with such pleasure on my time in the House of Commons makes it easier for me now to settle to new work. I have known people in the House of Commons stay until they've gone over the hill and people say, 'This chap isn't what he was three or four years ago.' There is nothing wrong in having twenty interesting years contributing to the life of the House of Commons and then feeling the attraction of an interesting job elsewhere.

Your background is almost a stereotype of a Conservative Minister.* You went to Eton and Christchurch and then entered the House of Commons and became a Minister. Was your choice of career determined by family and social background?

I think there is an illusion here. I didn't come from a political

*See note on pp. 57–8.

family particularly. My grandfather was an MP. My father wasn't and indeed, I am not sure my father would wholly have approved of me going into politics a year after I came down from university. Reading his diaries written in the last year or two of his life (he died just at the end of the war) I detect some doubt as to what was going to become of me in the next few years, and whether he was going to be happy about the direction I took. Again, mine was not the typical 'old Etonian' family. My father and I were the only two members of my family who ever went to Eton – my brother didn't and certainly none of his children will – so I think my career and home background look more stereotyped than they were. Also there was a formative time in my life which was the period between school and university. I still can't say much about that – it was wartime work that I think I'll still have to cloak under the general heading of 'Foreign Office'. But it enabled me to meet people whom I wouldn't have met at school, though I had a wide range of acquaintance at university also. But I think it was between 1942 and 1945 that I first became seriously interested in public affairs and it was then that I got into the habit of arguing them out with people, many of whom came from different backgrounds from myself and held diverse points of view.* I don't think I ever did seriously consider another career.

Could I press you a bit more on the first part of the question? What you are saying breaks the stereotype of the 'old Etonian' going into politics. Some political scientists would regard it as significant that a fairly large proportion of any Conservative Cabinet have this kind of background. You're saying that you are what you are and you're not a product of those determinants that sociologists would regard as typical to the making of a Conservative Minister?

Well, there's something in what they say. I recall when Keith Joseph and I both became Cabinet Ministers in 1962.† A former

* Boyle was eighteen in 1942.
†Sir Keith Joseph was Minister of Housing and Local Government in 1962. He has been Secretary of State for Health and Social Security since June 1970.

Conservative Under-Secretary said to me – someone from a different social background – 'Well, good luck to both of you and I think you both ought to do reasonably well, but it does seem almost too good a coincidence that you should both be baronets, one from Eton and one from Harrow.' I felt that was a perfectly fair comment. And of course, Eton always has been well represented in the Cabinet. The average income of Old Etonians is considerably higher than that of the nation at large and we probably do have more freedom to look around to consider what we'd like to do. But having said that, I think there is a danger of thinking too much in terms of stereotype and not enough of individual differences. After all, Eton has a College as well as the Oppidans. The best part of Eton is the College Foundation with its wide range of temperaments and views marked by extreme ability. Look at Harold Macmillan and contrast him with John Strachey and Freddie Ayer.* A wide range of intellectual brilliance, widely diverse in its application, has come out of the College.

At the time of Suez there were differences in the patterns of their behaviour between Old Etonians in the Cabinet; in that sort of situation Old Etonians are often found among the dissenters, I mean, Nutting and Nigel Nicolson, myself and Boothby, who would certainly be ranked rather strong dissenters at that time, were all Old Etonians.† Possibly it is that bit easier for us to dissent, I wouldn't deny this.

Becoming a Cabinet Minister

Politicians want to have an influence on affairs of state, perhaps to change the world. You were saying that it was the great social movements towards the end of the war, in the

---

*John Strachey was a Cabinet Minister in the 1945 Labour government and is well known for his writings on the theory of Socialism – *The Coming Struggle for Power* (Gollancz, 1932) is probably the best known.

†Anthony Nutting was Minister of State, Foreign Office, and resigned a few days before Edward Boyle in protest against Anthony Eden's Suez policy. Nigel Nicolson was Conservative Member for Bournemouth East and Christchurch until September 1959. He was not readopted by his constituency party because of his stand against the death penalty. Robert (now Lord) Boothby, former Conservative MP and well known for his independence of views and action, is now a cross-bench peer.

reports, and the thinking of the time, that attracted you to politics. But civil servants also have a major influence on policies. Why not aim to be a top civil servant, a Permanent Secretary rather than a Cabinet Minister, or an Assistant Secretary rather than an MP?*

It never occurred to me in the later years of the war or in the years immediately after 1945 that one might find it a rewarding career to become a civil servant – I knew terribly little about the civil service. If I had done, I think I might seriously have considered it. I would have worked harder at university to get a better degree and make this option possible.† One might even say that time has had its revenge here in the end because I think that a Vice-Chancellor of the University is more analogous to a Permanent Secretary than he is to a Minister.

But what are the real differences between politicians and civil servants? If you take civil servants whom we both knew – Nenk or Morrell – they were surely policy makers.‡ How can one differentiate these top-flight civil servants in their functions, in their interests and self-perception, from you and from Ministers of your calibre?

I think one important difference is that the top-level administrative civil servant – and it's a task that both Morrell and Nenk and also those who survive them like Toby Weaver and Jack Embling performed exceptionally well – identifies key issues for Ministers, orders the relevant facts and figures and sets out possible courses of action.** This is one of the most important jobs that civil servants perform for Ministers. Ministers, after all, are only Ministers because they are, in the first instance, politicans. They are Ministers because some-

*An Assistant Secretary is the first 'senior' rank in the administrative civil service.

†Edward Boyle took a third class in the History School at Oxford. How he managed this unspectacular feat must be a mystery to anybody who has discussed history with him.

‡See p. 29

**J. F. Embling is now Deputy Under-Secretary of State responsible for science policy in the DES.

body else has put them in that job. They have not graduated to it through the civil service through the judgement of their own equals. They've been put there by somebody. If they have creative imagination, as David Eccles did, they may become chiefly committed to – and identified with – certain policies, and of course it's their responsibility to sanction what is done. But it's not their first responsibility to identify the issues precisely and, of course, issues may come up which they wish hadn't. I think that this is one of the main jobs that a civil servant has. He must remind Ministers of the existence of some key issue whether the Minister's mind is focused on it at that moment or not.

How does this relate to definitions of policy making? Take David Easton's definition of policy as the authoritative allocation of values.* Or another definition that policy making is decision making on the basis of normative criteria, which is saying, in effect, that value-judgements are the essence of policy making, while the objective construction of their consequences is the essence of administration. You're saying, aren't you, that the value-judgements are not allocated strictly between Ministers and civil servants but that Ministers are different because they are authorized, licensed by the electoral process, to sanction the value-judgements?

Yes – you cannot make a judgement on economics, or education, or anything else, without implying a value-judgement of some kind. You can't have any argument about what is best for the nation without implying the criteria of the word 'best'. And, equally important, you may be implying certain value-judgements that you are only half aware of yourself. About the distribution of the national income – this takes one back to the old controversy about how an unwillingness to plan is, itself, a form of planning. Indeed, I think this is one respect in which all my political life I found myself athwart one part of Tory ideology. I remember Robert Nield saying to me 'I always feel that with you, you are looking for the value-judgement as the joker in the pack', and I think that's quite true.† I've never

*D. Easton, *The Political System*, Knopf, 1953.
†See p. 18.

been somebody who has found it easy to conceive that there could be a sort of norm of right thinking. People differ in their values and you've got to be honest with yourself and other people about this. Ministers are appointed with a party background. They belong with a party as well as to a government and they are appointed with the responsibility of making clear what their value-judgements are. I think, though, there are three reservations I'd make to the formulation as you've put it. The first is that Ministers are never, or seldom, masters of circumstances to the extent they like to think. Mistakes are often made by governments or by Ministers when they think of themselves as more master of circumstances than in fact they are. You must recognize the constraints within which you operate and see them clearly. Perhaps this is the most conservative side of my thinking. You've got to start with what you've got. Secondly, while it is the responsibility of the Minister to make his preferences clear and to be frank about his value-judgements, and to remember that excellent phrase of Mendès-France, *Gouverner c'est choisir,** it's the Minister's job to choose, and no government can shirk the business of choosing. Even so, it's unreal to suppose that in any dialogue between Ministers and civil servants, the civil servants' value-judgements won't play some part as well. All of us imply values in whatever we say: that applies to civil servants, too, and it's no enlargement of their function, it's no false attribution to recognize that they also have their own preferences which will out in discussion. Finally, there is Edward Crankshaw's distinction between conflicts of ambition and conflicts of conviction.† A great deal of in-fighting in governments – battles between, say, a Ministry and the Treasury – sometimes resolve themselves eventually into conflicts of ambition; you want to have so much; the Treasury wants you to have half that; you finally decide to settle for somewhere in between the two. A good many conflicts of ambition of that kind play a considerable part in collective argument

*Pierre Mendès-France was Prime Minister of France from June 1954 to February 1955.

†Edward Crankshaw is Soviet Affairs Correspondent of the *Observer* and the author of several books on Eastern Europe.

in government, though, of course, unless you have strong convictions to start with, the outcome of the battle won't be likely to be favourable – Treasury Ministers soon get to know who are those of their colleagues who really care. One more point occurs to me. I think the interplay between Ministers and civil servants works most successfully when their views are instinctively neither too close nor too far apart Often the best partnership comes when the head of a Department holds broadly the same philosophy as the government, but has important reservations. Then he will be listened to.

What effect does insecurity have on the thinking of the politician? It obviously affects his judgement on priorities, doesn't it? Working within a pattern of insecurity might make a difference between the pace at which the Minister and his civil servants move towards objectives. It might also affect the range of the objectives. The Minister is in power for too short a time. Does it mean that you feel you have to act quickly?

I think some people feel this. I must say, I didn't particularly, myself, as a Minister. When I became Minister of Education in 1962, it looked as though my party would probably lose the General Election in 1964, as narrowly they did. But as against the fact that I might only be in power for a year or two, the political situation equally made it unlikely that I would be reshuffled away from Education before the election took place. I wasn't tremendously conscious of hustle, of a time scale. Indeed, I felt sometimes that one or two officials felt it rather than myself. I can remember, for example, early in 1964 I think, the Roman Catholics from the North-West writing to me about secondary organization as it affected them, and one official in the Department putting up a minute to me which said, practically, in these words, 'Presumably the Minister will feel ...' (I am not sure that he even put it as politely as that) 'that this isn't a matter that he ought to take a very firm decision about at this stage of the political cycle.' I remember being a little surprised to find the words 'at this stage of the political cycle' on the minute. By the end of my time there were one or two other officials more conscious than I of the fact that a change of government was probably imminent.

I've always believed as a Minister that clearing the 'In-tray' is not the only job. Certainly, one has got to be all the time looking ahead, identifying issues, fighting for resources; but dealing with requests, simply dealing with the 'In-tray', is one pretty important part of being a Minister and I think I dealt with it in much the same way in 1963 and 1964 as if my party had just come into power.

Most Ministers have an average tenure within any one Department of about two years – that's fairly general. Denis Healey had six years at Defence, which is unusual.* If one contrasts that time span with that of, say, Swedish social democratic educational planning, in which there were five years of research by Husèn and the rest, then a five-year period in which they matched schools in Stockholm to see how comprehensivization worked, and then a change of law and then a ten-year plan concerted between the Royal Swedish Board of Education and the Ministry of Finance to get the thing off the ground, this was, in fact, a cycle of twenty years over which a major piece of social engineering was achieved, and through all of that time there was continuity of political leadership and administration. How can one say that a Minister such as yourself, given two or three years, perhaps, in a Department such as Education, could measure up to that process of long-term formation of objectives? You talk about the 'In-tray' – aren't you really dealing with the top of the 'In-tray', rather than the nasty, faded carbons at the bottom of it that contain the long-term issues, if you're in for so short a period of time?

I think this really comes back to Lord Salisbury's famous remark that he was never too weighed down as Prime Minister by the burden of responsibility, but he did feel the burden of decision, whether it was on a great matter or a small; how you decided it simply depended on the materials available. I always thought there was much to be said for that philosophy. Now, one thing I think a Minister should always do when dealing with a big issue like secondary school reorganization,

*He was Minister of Defence for the whole period of the Wilson government, October 1964 – June 1970.

that clearly is not finally going to be decided in a short time, is to take a decision that leaves the maximum of options open for the future. I never had much sympathy with an authority, or, more likely, perhaps, a Conservative Opposition in authority, who said 'Don't approve this school, because it could be operated as a comprehensive with another school in two or three years' time.' I used to express just the opposite view; planning schools in such a way as to leave the maximum of options open to the future was a good thing to do, since clearly this was a subject that was going to be with us for a good many years. I remember when I first discovered as Minister in 1963 that no fewer than ninety local education authorities had reorganization plans. One of the historical myths is that comprehensive reorganization all started with *Circular 10/65*.* It didn't. It started a number of years before. We felt at the Ministry in 1963 that we must be in a position not to tell authorities what plan to go for, but give them some kind of broad guidance about certain kinds of plans. It became perfectly clear that we would have to have some changes in the law to allow middle schools so that you didn't have to change from primary to secondary at the age of ten or eleven.† In fact, as soon as the 1964 election was announced, I got on to the Prime Minister and asked if we could please have that Bill which would legalize middle schools? This was arranged without much difficulty and I suppose you might call the 1964 Act my parting gift to the Ministry. And one of the reasons why I never felt able to take quite so strong a position against *Circular 10/65* as some of my supporters would have liked, was that I knew the spadework leading up to that circular was the result of the replies to an inquiry that I had sanctioned in

*See p. 62, n. 31.

†The Education Act, 1964, allowed local authorities to establish schools that cut across existing definitions of 'primary' and 'secondary' education. It had been necessary to establish this difference firmly in the 1944 Act to get rid of all-age schools. By the early 1960s many in the education service were arguing in favour of three stages of education – first schools from five to eight or nine years, middle schools from eight or nine to twelve or thirteen years, upper schools from twelve or thirteen to eighteen years. The arguments for the different schemes are discussed in ch. 10 of the *Plowden Report*.

1963. So one does know as a Minister a number of subjects are going to be with us for a long time, but I would still say I never felt too oppressed by this. The only sensible line to take was to assume you had all the time in the world, and that – to use a cricket analogy – there was no crisis except the next ball. Take the most sensible decision you can on all the points that come to you, but don't close options for the future.

Hugh Dalton, in his memoirs, quotes Arthur Henderson as saying, 'The first forty-eight hours decide whether a Minister is going to run his office, or whether his office is going to run him,' and Dalton himself said that a Minister should show his officials at the start that he has a mind of his own.* Do you share this view?

I think that's one of those remarks, like Burke's letter to the electors of Bristol, which may get overquoted in books on politics.† In the same way, that remark in Dalton's volume should be quoted in its context, which was the almost incredible folly of putting before Arthur Henderson on his first day as Foreign Secretary a suggestion that he should congratulate the Pope on the Lateran Treaty he had just made with Mussolini. Anything more idiotic to put before a devoted old-style north-country Wesleyan you could hardly imagine, and I don't think many civil servants would be so silly as that today. I would have thought it was more important in the early days for the civil servants to be clear whether they can have confidence in their Minister or not. Lady Sharpe recently said some things about this which I think are right.‡ Civil servants

*See p. 62, n. 29.

†Boyle went on: 'Edmund Burke's remark should never be quoted without a reference to its context which is that there were few Public Bills in the eighteenth century but a large number of Private Bills, particularly affecting ports.' In 1774 Burke dissented from his fellow MP for Bristol who had promised to be bound by all the instructions of his constituents – at that time a quite common practice. (See W. S. Holdsworth, *History of English Law*, Methuen, 1938, vol. 10, pp. 597–600.) 'Your representative owes you, not his industry only, but his judgement; and he betrays, instead of serving you, if he sacrifices it to your judgement. This is the difference between a delegate and a representative.'

‡Baroness Sharpe, formerly Dame Evelyn Sharpe, was Permanent Secretary to the Ministry of Housing and Local Government. Her remarks

want to know whether their Minister is going to be one of those who tends to get his way when there is collective discussion. Is he going to be one who knews clearly what he wants, what he's going after, and one whose reactions they can, on most cases, correctly anticipate? Those are important questions and civil servants will quite soon become aware of the answers to them. But the idea that there's a sort of tussle of power on the first afternoon and that it's vital for the Minister to win it is an oversimplification.

Don't civil servants reckon they have in trust the ongoing work and policies of the Department? Given a feeble Minister, rather than one who will get his way the civil servant will make sure that disaster doesn't overtake the area for which they are responsible. Is this putting it too strongly?

No, I think that is true. I think it is also true that a rather capricious Minister, or one who doesn't seem quite to know his own mind, will soon have a bad effect on the morale of the Department. Departments make up or compensate for the deficiencies of their Ministers remarkably well but. oh dear, some Ministers really can lower morale very quickly and easily.

A succession of weak Ministers can cause a Department to run out of gas?

Quite true. This is really saying that each side has got to do its job. The Minister has the absolute responsibility for showing what he's going for, to make clear what he is going for, how he wants to play the hand, and what are to him the most important objectives. The officials have got the equally important job of helping him by identifying the issues correctly. The idea that there's a sort of ju-jitsu game on arrival, and that it's absolutely essential for a Minister to win the very first day, is taking one's eye off things that are more important, and, as I say, the episode that prompted this remark in Dalton's book I don't think would often arise these days.

are quoted in the *Listener*, 1 October 1970. Anthony Crosland makes the same point on p. 167.

On Being a Minister

On one famous evening in 1962 Mr Macmillan sacked seven members of his Cabinet and you became Minister of Education. Overnight you ceased to be Financial Secretary to the Treasury and became, for the first time, the senior Minister of a major Department of State. You must have been familiar with the main policies and problems of the education service because you had been Parliamentary Secretary there on your return to the government after the Suez crisis. Did you have any clear views on the educational policies that you wanted to put into effect?

Well, there was one issue immediately before us at that time. I knew all about it from the Treasury end as well as the Curzon Street end. The very morning of the sackings, we'd had a discussion in a Cabinet Committee about teacher supply and the further expansion of the teacher training colleges. We took that extraordinary decision in 1957 in the government to go over to the three-year course with no increase in training-college places and I remember you saying to me, as my Private Secretary, how odd a decision that would seem. And then we shortly afterwards had a further twelve thousand places – and then four thousand more, and then after the *Crowther Report*, after a great deal of battling between the Ministry and the Treasury, eight thousand more again.* Then there was this further recommendation of the National Advisory Council on the Training and Supply of Teachers which had come up in the summer of 1962,† and this was causing a good deal of controversy between Curzon Street and the Treasury. I arrived at Curzon Street knowing that I would immediately have to deal with this and that I would be changing sides abruptly. I raised this matter with my Cabinet colleagues before the end of July. Mr Macmillan told me afterwards he thought I

*Boyle must be referring here to the decision to raise the school-leaving age to sixteen in 1970 which was recommended by the Crowther Committee; see pp. 47 and 60, n. 13.

†National Advisory Council, *Report on Demand and Supply, 1960–1980*, (England), H M S O, 1962.

presented it quite sensibly. I didn't press for a decision that July. It seemed better to leave it for a few more months. I also thought the terms of the NAC's recommendation were not quite right and that rather than go on having this metaphysics about 'crowded' and 'uncrowded' places, it would be better to aim at a target of student places.* As you may remember, we got a completely satisfactory decision in January 1963 – it was a pushover. We got the decision to go up initially to sixty-five thousand and then to eighty thousand places in the colleges, which was a big expansion. That's what I remember most about my transfer from the Treasury to the Ministry of Education. I had abruptly to change sides on a costly issue where the case wasn't altogether easy to argue because we had this high rate of wastage among women teachers, but nonetheless one had to do battle – it was a matter of deciding how to play the hand wisely. And then, of course, there were other issues which I knew were bound to come up. Notably, the issue of the 11-plus and secondary reorganization, and I knew there would also be battles about the school building programme. Looking back on it, I'm not sure I was quite wise in my decision to press the Treasury all the way on the teacher supply point, but not so much over school building. I remember consciously taking that decision and, of course, this turned out right in the end because the following year we got a good building programme with a high level of school improvements for the two years after that. It isn't so much the broad philosophy as one particular contested issue which is there and then on your plate.

May I supplement that answer by checking with you the process by which the earliest of these decisions was taken? The Registrar-General had produced a report showing that there was a change in birth rate which would affect the school population. The data reached the Department through the Accountant-General at the time, who immediately got to work

---

*The DES planners had to decide whether to press for expansion on the assumption that colleges could continue to be as 'crowded' or whether they could assume that students would be housed at the approved standards.

with Miles-Davies, the Under-Secretary in charge of teacher training and teacher supply. A meeting under the Permanent Secretary, Gilbert Flemming, was then convened, which I seem to remember lasted all morning, and a decision of officials was made right away to advise Ministers that a change of policy was necessary. David Eccles had up to that time been defending the position to keep a static control figure for teacher training numbers on the grounds that the present number would be sufficient and that an increase in training plant would cause teacher unemployment in the late 1960s, but Geoffrey Lloyd and you then had to make a decision very quickly indeed to seek a change in policy from the Treasury and the Cabinet.

Yes, that was it.

You had no difficulty in finding your way around the Department as other Ministers might have found, and as senior Minister there you had supreme authority within the Department. How did you perceive your role in terms of the civil servants whom you knew but to whom you now had to relate as a senior, rather than as a junior Minister?

I was struck by the extent to which the Department had changed since I had been there before – between 1959 and 1962. There was, of course, a new Permanent Secretary, and two exceptionally able and powerful Deputy Secretaries, Toby Weaver and Antony Part, who didn't always hold the same views. They'd been Under-Secretaries before and now they were both Deputy Secretaries, whereas there had only been one Deputy Secretary when I was there before. You had certain parts of the Ministry, like the Youth Service Branch, which was stronger; and two Further Education Branches, where there had been one before. What I came back to had been strengthened by David Eccles in his second term of office. I recall that I was behind Ministry thinking on a number of subjects. For example, in 1958 on the whole the Department thought it was better to keep the percentage of grammar school places down so as to encourage the modern schools to build up their GCE courses.* By 1962 in Schools Branch there was much more of a propensity to think that even with separate schools there must be a reasonable and, if necessary, a rising proportion of grammar school places. I noticed a criticism recently that I never realized the need for more grammar school places, for more O level places in academic schools. This in fact was not true. After 1962, I consciously moved away with the encouragement of Schools Branch from the doctrine that had been current since about 1958. And, of course, there was a growing feeling in Schools Branch that more comprehensives were quite certainly coming along. Departments are changing all the time. The landscape, the way in which issues are regarded, the assumptions behind policy, are all the time changing just a bit. There's nothing like returning as a Minister to a Department for realizing how fallacious it is to assume that presuppositions, on the whole, remain the same.

This says something about the nature of bureaucracy as well. The assumption that there are predetermined and static suppositions within bureaucracy is nonsense.

Absolute and dangerous nonsense, if only because new officials are coming to positions of authority and their value-judgements, as we said just now, are a factor in the situation as well. Few of us see a range of facts in exactly the same way as each other. Sometimes the same facts add up the same way for most of us, probably with regard to apartheid, say, but this is not as often as people think in a liberal democracy. The relative importance we attach to the important issues varies and we create our own models of reality. Of course it's right that social science should generalize but if I wanted to generalize on British public affairs, I would lay the biggest emphasis on the very large number of individual views on facts that are held at any one time. I was strongly conscious of that when Minister.

You have modestly evaded one of the points in a previous question. You left the Department as an honoured Parlia-

*This involves persuading pupils to stay beyond the compulsory school-leaving age – then fifteen years.

mentary Secretary. You came back as boss. What was the difference?

Well, of course, there is a great difference. Education is one of those subjects where the personality of the Minister, the way he intends to play it, counts for a great deal. In a sense he's got to stand a little apart from his colleagues, he's got to fight all the time for the interests of the service about which they won't all be well informed.

Are you differentiating here between Education and some other Ministries?

I can think of some Departments where a Minister might have ideas about policy but he's not the person who has to champion the service as at Education, or the person who other people will want to attack when things go wrong. This is the contrast between, say, Education and the Ministry of Works, or even the Minister in charge of local government affairs. And I'm not sure that at, say, Transport – a subject on which people feel strongly – you're looked on as the person whose job it is to be the champion of the service in quite the same way. I think, perhaps, Agriculture is one of the nearest analogies to Education.

Is that possibly because Education has a higher ideological content than, say, the Ministry of Works?

Well partly that, but partly, I think, for this reason. Education is always going to be a thorn in the flesh of the Chancellor of the Exchequer. It's something that always costs, not just more money but really significantly more money than you're expecting. I can remember David Eccles getting into trouble with some of his colleagues for saying in January 1960 that education would be costing the nation fourteen hundred million a year in the early 1970s.* Well, of course, in fact he was quite wrong, but by underestimating and not by overestimating it. But this is a service which is bound to be

*'For the first time . . . the education budget stands at over £2000 million, exceeds defence, and is taking nearly 6 per cent of the gross national product.' Brian MacArthur, *Education for the Seventies*, Heinemann, 1970.

unpopular with the Chancellor – it always costs more. I remember our admirable Finance Officer, Jack Embling, saying, 'You know what the Treasury sometimes say about us is that we are never quite sure what we want except that it is always more,' and there is truth in that (though I do think we knew what we wanted).* What makes it more difficult is that you're arguing and fighting for this service to a large extent with people who don't know, haven't experienced its real inwardness, and many of whom have had no experience of maintained schools, and for that matter, no experience of civic universities. I think this is why the personality of the Minister and whether he is really prepared to discover the inwardness of the service, and champion it, is felt by the educational world to be of particular importance.

It is true, isn't it, that both you and such junior Ministers as Christopher Chataway were able to make a distinctive mark on the educational service, even as junior Ministers?† Some would say that junior Ministers haven't really got a job to do. What was your role when you were Parliamentary Secretary to the Ministry of Education? Did you do anything to strengthen that position when you became Secretary of State?

I agree with you that there's a tendency in the press to exaggerate the importance of the junior Minister. Whenever a new batch of junior Ministers is appointed, we always have this solemn comment on who they are, and whether they are promising or not. This is mostly crap. There are few Departments where any normally intelligent Parliamentarian couldn't do the junior job all right. There were far too many junior Ministers appointed by the Labour government – top civil servants had great difficulty in finding anything for them to do. Now, Education, as you and I will remember when we were together, wasn't quite like that. There was a certain amount of Parliamentary and lowish-level administrative work – opposition to compulsory purchase orders, morally unsatisfactory teachers, the special schools, which were interesting, and a certain amount of case work for secondary reorganization.

*See p. 73.   †See p. 46.

Geoffrey Lloyd, when he was Minister, let me do all that.* I
hope I did the same with Chris Chataway. I think I left him all
the administrative work of that kind and of course he was exceptionally good at it. Another thing which I was careful of
where Chris was concerned – I think this is important – whenever there was a Bill going through Parliament which involved
the Ministry of Education, like the London Government Bill,
or the Industrial Training Bill, Chris was the spokesman on
the Standing Committee, so that he got at any rate a reasonable share of the Parliamentary work – some of it quite tax-
ing.† Otherwise there aren't normally many Parliamentary
debates for the Parliamentary Secretary – not more than one
major debate a year, though a lot of adjournment debates. I
think it was quite interesting as junior jobs go; you could do
quite a bit of visiting local authorities – if they couldn't get
the Minister, the Parliamentary Secretary was quite a reasonably acceptable substitute in most of the local education authorities. The educational world was not beastly to its Parliamentary Secretaries – if the Minister for any reason couldn't
come, the junior Minister was welcome.

Could I remind you of a conversation we had a few weeks
after you came to the Department? It was quite obvious that
the role of the Parliamentary Secretary was, in the first place,
not terribly well defined, and secondly, wasn't going to provide an enormous amount of work for someone of your
capacity and ability. We had a long discussion about what the
Parliamentary Secretary in Education ought to do. I think that
the analogy that we both hit on was that of Sir Samuel Hoare
in the early 1920s, who felt strongly that the Royal Air Force
was going to be an important part of the defence system,
and that the thing that it lacked above all was Ministerial
backing, and reputation and status in the whole coun-

* Geoffrey Lloyd was Minister of Education, 1957–9.
†These Bills were both remitted to Standing Committees for committee
study. At this point in the procedure, the discussion is relatively informal,
detailed and technical and although it rarely attracts public notice is a part
of Parliamentary activity when Ministers are quite severely tested. Junior
ministers usually make most of the official speeches and have to be available
to defend details throughout the proceedings.

try.* You felt that any Minister who could make known to the wider political community the merits, advantages, problems and policies of the education service would be doing an important job. And so you took upon yourself the task of going to the country, of extolling the virtues of the system, and of bringing it home to the people who helped to form opinion. Is that a correct account of how you saw at least part of your role as Parliamentary Secretary?

Yes, absolutely correct. And I don't remember, if I could help it, ever refusing a request from a local authority to pay a visit.

And you enjoyed doing it, even though it meant long train journey at the end of quite a long Parliamentary week?

Yes, I did. And of course, if you come up through the other system, like me, you did want to learn about the maintained schools and these visits did teach you a lot. There was also the enormous advantage of having London close at hand. Looking back on it, I think I learned more from visiting schools than anywhere else. Of all the great cities in the world, London is the one that doesn't have disastrous breakdowns and does have some very good schools. The thing that was the most unfamiliar world to me, and I had to learn a great deal about, was the further education system. We ought, perhaps, to remember that in those days the Ministry never had responsibility for the universities, but there was the whole range of the technical colleges. The CATs had only just been designated (in fact they hadn't all been designated) and the whole system of CATs and regional technical colleges, area technical colleges, local colleges – they had only just been set up in David Eccles's White Paper of 1956.† Learning about all that and speaking coherently about it in the House of Commons was a great difficulty. Do you remember the mess I got into preparing for my first Parliamentary debate in, I should say, March 1957? I remember it as one of the few occasions when I felt quite ashamed of myself because a civil servant

*See p. 56.

†All the colleges of advanced technology have since become techological universities following the recommendations of the *Robbins Report*. For David Eccles's White Paper on technical education see p. 20.

really had to sort out my speech, unpick it almost from the beginning to the end; I simply wasn't seeing the subject coherently at all without a good deal of work beforehand.

This must again be one of the differentiators between civil service roles and Ministers' roles? The visits had a purpose. Ministers can set the tone and create the attitudes in the community towards the education service. You won't like the word, but the 'evangelical' role, the building up of opinion and sentiment behind the service, is something for Ministers and politicians, rather than for civil servants.

Yes, it is also, of course, important to do it skilfully; and particularly when you're new and enthusiastic you can easily force your voice, put it in the wrong way. I am always struck with the tremendous difficulties of communication in our society. Putting the case for educational expansion in such a way as to get favourable notice in the local press, rather than a critical notice, is just as important as having the right 'evangelical' urges.

You gave an example before of one policy you had to get right as you came into office. What about the other nine or ten major issues that must have passed through your office when you were Minister? Where did these policies come from? Were they generated by Conservative Central Office, or by Party Conferences? Were they the result of Cabinet determination? Did the Prime Minister stimulate any of them? Were MPs getting at you to put the different policies through? Did they come from your own head? Where is policy generated?

Well, in Education, and I think this is the difference between education and some other subjects, I would say overwhelmingly the biggest number originated from what one broadly calls the 'education world', if you like, from the logic of the education service as it was developing. Teacher supply, which we've mentioned, well, that was something everybody was concerned about, but it was the National Advisory Council who were looking at it, as it were, a bit more scientifically, and it was the local authorities that were concerned with

staffing the schools. Issues like secondary school reorganization, the 11-plus, to some extent were becoming popular issues
but I would say, mostly, the starting point for educational
questions was the education world itself. Not the Prime Minister to any great extent, who after all had never been Minister
of Education.* (David Eccles said to me: 'You will find it
difficult to get the Cabinet to understand education because
so few of them have been involved in the maintained schools').
There were Mr Butler and Lord Hailsham, to help in Cabinet
but the Prime Minister had never been in that office.† While I
always had a sympathetic treatment from Mr Macmillan
about education, it was obvious that he'd lived with housing
in a way he'd never lived with the education service.‡ The
Party Conference did not produce much, though the first debate I had to answer at the Party Conference in October 1962
was a debate calling for the expansion of higher education.
Now that voices, usually hailing from All Souls, or wherever,
are saying that Robbins was a great mistake, and that this
concentration on the numbers of qualified students was, and
is, a great mistake, it is worth recalling the pressure there was
in the early 1960s to expand higher education. This pressure
was felt in the Party Conference itself.

Of course one could say that higher education is a very good
form of consumption expenditure and well within the Opportunity State frame of reference. But you are saying that
education itself largely generates policy. At the same time, a
decision on teacher supply is contingent on a decision to raise
the school leaving age, or a decision to increase the length of
teacher training, or a decision to put more resources into
education for deprived children. All of these are determined
within larger political frames of reference than the education
service itself. They can't simply be generated by the education
service itself, surely?

*Harold Macmillan and Sir Alec Douglas-Home were the Prime
Ministers during Boyle's Ministry.

†R. A. (now Lord) Butler and Lord Hailsham were both former Ministers of
Education.

‡Harold Macmillan was Minister of Housing and Local Government,
1951 to 1954.

I was really answering your question 'Where did the policies come from when I first became Minister?' I think at that time, in 1962, it was still the education world that was in the lead here. It was from that area that most of the pressures came or were focused at that time.

What about the external intelligentsia: for example, Vaizey, and the educational sociologists, Floud, Halsey and so on, who helped shape the new thinking of the 1960s?*

I think again this was most marked about 1963 onwards. This was one respect in which the world of 1962–3 was different from the world of the 1950s. The work of these people made one realize that the pool of potential ability was deeper than we'd thought, and that the interplay between nature and nurture was more subtle than used to be accepted. I think, though, to some extent it was the reports of 1963 that finally clinched it. Perhaps Robbins, more than Newsom, because Robbins did put this so explicitly. It's interesting that the report dealing with what one might think the most glamorous and elitist part of the service was most outspoken on this subject, pointing out the small proportion of wage-earning families whose children got to university. After 1963 it was hardly controversial to say that you had massive evidence of the numbers of boys and girls who were being allowed to write themselves off below their true level of ability. I think 1963 was a watershed here, Newsom and Robbins both coming out in that year. It was those reports that really cemented the work that the educational sociologists had done in the previous years. I remember in Professor Bantock's book *Education and Values* he said, 'Anyone of real ability can now make the grade, if that is the word for it', and I remember thinking you mightn't have been surprised to see that in the 1950s; it did seem a very unexpected thing to read in a serious book about education in 1965. If you'd had any deep experience of the education world did you on the whole agree with Professor Bantock that any person with real ability could make the grade, or did you want to stand with the *Robbins Report* that there was a great deal of potential ability still there, if we were

*See p. 24.

willing to help it? I would have thought the norm of opinion by '65 was clearly on Robbins's side and not on Bantock's. And this I think was a very important change in the history of education. Indeed I would like to think, if I contributed anything to education, or indeed anything at all during my twenty years in politics, I did something to bring 'middle' opinion over to this side, to make it plain that the norm of opinion had shifted here and that middle opinion had just simply got to accommodate itself to this.

The 11-plus system, the emphasis on the G-factor and intelligence were the egalitarianism of the 1920s and 1930s – a way of selecting the 'able poor'. It was really the educational sociologists who showed that as measured in terms of people who got the benefits from the system, this could not be true.* Also such Swedish researchers as Husén were really attacking the reliability of this type of testing as a technical system of devices.† So by the 1950s there were already arguments which were showing that the 'weak' concept of equality was not good enough if one really wanted equality.‡ One had, at the same time, Vaizey and the rest joining in with Floud and Halsey, to show that the selective system was a poor distributor towards the able poor, simply as a system of distributing benefits. And these two things were going on through the 1950s so that by the time you came to the 1960s you could get your preface to Newsom which said, 'The essential point is that all children should have an equal opportunity of acquiring intelligence, and developing their talents and abilities to the full.' This was a massive doctrine for a Minister, and above all a Conservative Minister, to be writing as a preface to a CAC report. And secondly, the enshrining of that doctrine in policy by the virtually instantaneous acceptance of the *Robbins Report* by the Home Cabinet, which was, after all accepting social demand as a policy criterion. Was it, then, between the early fifties and the early nineteen-sixties, that this great transition

*See p. 24.　　†See p. 23.

‡See p. 51. This terminology was devised by Anthony Crosland in *The Future of Socialism*.

took place – beginning with the intelligentsia, the sociologists, the educational psychologists, the economists who created a climate of opinion that ten years later a radical Conservative, such as yourself, was able to confirm as policy?

That puts it fairly. Can I just put two glosses on that? The first is about Robbins. I think one of the reasons why the government accepted Robbins so quickly – and there were a number of interesting reasons for this – is that the government had always had a bad conscience about 1962, about the quarrel with the UGC over a level of recurrent grants and also about university pay at that time.* One thing that I think is underrated sometimes is when governments take a decision which is a bad one, and a hard one to defend, they often more than compensate for it in the next round, as it were. In fairness to the Macmillan government, and in fairness to the Treasury of which I was then a member, we reversed that bad decision pretty quickly, I remember. The quarrel with the UGC was made up by the Autumn of 1962, but I think echoes of this dispute were among the reasons that caused the government to accept Robbins with such alacrity. And, of course, a number of us knew, including Lord Hailsham, who was always on the side of expansion in the universities, that competition for university entry had been a problem for the schools for many years since the *Crowther Report* appeared in 1959. On the other point, I was perfectly aware that my words about people having more equal opportunities to 'acquire intelligence' were not original. Whether they were originally Tony Crosland's or whether we both got them from John Vaizey, I am not absolutely certain. But they were the words 'in the air' at that time. I do remember the original draft that was put up to me as a preface to Newsom and I remember saying to several people, including our then Press Officer, Noel Cowen, 'Look, this point about the need for a stronger doctrine of equality of opportunity – the need for young people to have more equal opportunities to acquire intelligence – this seems to me both true and important. Now isn't the

*Grants made every five years for running expenses. Capital grants for buildings are the other main type of grant.

preface to Newsom a good occasion for giving, so to speak, official endorsement to this point of view?' It was somebody else's doctrine, but I alone, at that moment, was in a position to give official blessing to it and that was the point of the preface.

How heavily did the responsibilities of being Secretary of State, or Minister, weigh on you? To the outside world you were responsible for all the major decisions and had to defend them. If this was so, how did you keep up with all of this work?

Well, the responsibility did weigh rather heavily on me. Incidentally, I think it's here that Salisbury's distinction between the burden of decision and the burden of responsibility slightly breaks down, because if the decisions had just been my decisions, it wouldn't have been so difficult. The most difficult aspect of the job is that so many decisions rely on collective discussions with colleagues. There are few important educational decisions that don't involve money, don't involve discussions with the Treasury and deciding how to play the hand – at what moment to put on the greatest amount of pressure in your dealings with the Treasury Ministers. As someone who hadn't been a full Minister before, I did find these a considerable burden. Many of the issues didn't worry me too much – such as secondary reorganization. I had no doubt that separate schools at eleven over the next few years would be increasingly on the way out. I had no doubt that it was going to be more difficult to defend making different arrangements for children at the age of eleven across an arbitrary borderline. It became a matter of how you put it, how you expressed your policy. I made something of a new departure at the AEC Conference of 1963,* when I said we could no longer look upon separate schools at eleven as the norm and look on anything else as experimental. And although one mustn't read history backwards, I think the sort of argument that I so often found myself rehearsing in the years after 1965, had begun to take shape in my mind before 1963. In other words I didn't find it difficult to take day-to-day administrative decisions. It was the decisions that involved collective discussions with my col-

*Association of Education Committees Conference.

leagues that I found the hardest. And one has got to look at this against the background of all the other Cabinet work. If you're a Cabinet Minister, you've got all the other big issues like the Common Market and other, much more disagreeable intrusions, like Profumo, all coming in at the same time. You've got your work on Cabinet Committees, the Home Affairs Committee and the Economic Policy Committee, too – I was always a member of the EPC during my years as a Minister.

In simple terms – did you ever lose a night's sleep over any of the decisions you had to take as a Secretary of State?

I can't remember actually losing a night's sleep. I think I'm more inclined to get cross with myself about tactically handling matters badly and when I do it's nearly always been mistakes of omission rather than mistakes of commission. For instance, at the time of the dispute over teachers' salaries I did not check with my constituency agent that one or two, as it were, unscripted confrontations wouldn't take place. I think I'm somebody who has always been reasonably good at meetings when I'm prepared for them. I've never been good at suddenly being confronted by an unexpected situation. I'm not a good improviser. I was more apt to stay awake for an extra half hour on post mortems than I would on the burden of responsibility to be taken the following day.

The most comfortable way round, anyway. There is pressure on Ministers to make instant decisions.* Did you find this uncomfortable, or frightening, or just plain bad as a way of governing or running a system? What chance does any government have of taking its time about a major decision? The present Prime Minister, on coming into office, made quite a thing of this.

Well, I think he's dead right there. Of course, the particular one I was talking about, the question of teacher supply, I did, in fact, manage to put off the crucial decision until January, and then we got a satisfactory outcome. I always tried to avoid coming to instant decisions. It's quite extraordinary, though, how cabinets do make them. Looking back on Cabinet meetings,

*See pp. 43 and 155–6.

how often we would get on to something quite important at ten to one and would settle that by one o'clock. One or two decisions did come up which we settled in Cabinet in ten minutes, and I think somebody ought to have said, 'Look, this really is rather important and, whoever's right or wrong about this, I think we ought to give careful thought to it before reaching a conclusion.'

This puts into question the Cabinet as a good instrument for taking major policy desisions. Obviously there has to be some such mechanism, but is it not unrealistic to rely simply on the Cabinet meeting as the main point of convergence of government?

I think you've got always to remember the particular situation. The period I'm thinking of, January 1963, was one where we'd just had the shock over the breakdown of the Common Market negotiations. There was a tendency to feel that you really mustn't take a decision unwelcome to the Treasury too often. Whatever anybody may say now, anything to do with pay, and percentage increases in pay, were always controversial matters throughout the later years of the Conservative government. The idea that any government can get on without some sort of incomes policy seems to me quite unreal. And therefore there are all kinds of reasons why that kind of decision tends to be taken rather quickly. I think it's one of the marks of a good Cabinet that there are enough members who will say, 'Let's fasten our seat belts before we take off, let's be absolutely clear we've thought through what the implications are of this.' The decision about post office wages in 1964 was taken pretty quickly.* What a good thing it would have been, looking back on it, if someone had said in the early months of 1964, 'But look, are we really going to be able to see this through?' When Cabinets are under pressure they don't always spend the amount of time they should looking several moves ahead.

*A reference to the GPO decision to allow wages to go beyond the government's 'guiding light' of $3\frac{1}{2}$ per cent, and the government's reluctant acceptance of this because of growing pressure for increases in other parts of the public sector.

How did you spend your day or week as Secretary of State?

There is nothing like politics for appearing to be always busy while not doing very much and I noticed a big difference when I came to Leeds as Vice-Chancellor. My day seems to be much more concentrated and better organized here. I didn't start my day early enough, looking back on it, and I think a lot of other Ministers made the same mistake. I wasn't due in the office, as you will recall, before 10 o'clock – this was the time when the Home Affairs Committee met. I start the day here fairly punctually at 9 o'clock and that is much better. I suspect Labour are sometimes better at starting the day earlier than Conservative Ministers.

We do both know one Minister who started his day at 1 p.m.

Yes, but he was exceptional. But if you asked me what I did, well of course there were the ordinary office meetings, not all that many chores, because I left a lot of them to Chris Chataway – as much to him as Geoffrey Lloyd left to me – but there was always seeing a good many people, representatives from teachers, representatives from local authority associations. I shouldn't think there were many weeks when I didn't see either Sir Ronald Gould or Sir William Alexander about something, deputations from local authorities about school building, and so on. Then, of course, there were the Ministers' meetings. I was in Cabinet on Tuesdays and Thursdays, which immobilized two mornings completely, and another day when we had Economic Policy Committee at 10 o'clock, which usually went on for more than an hour. Therefore, Cabinets and Cabinet Committees took a good deal of time. There were a certain number of other Ministers' meetings as well; when Sir Alec Douglas-Home became Prime Minister he asked me to be on the Rhodesia Committee, for example. And then, of course, in the afternoon I quite often had to be at the House of Commons – I don't think I very often went down for no other purpose than listening to a debate. And then, at weekends, of course, there were the visits to local authorities, also visits to the constituency.

Again, I think you've put this rather modestly. Would I be

right in guessing that from 10 o'clock in the morning till 10 o'clock at night when you were likely to be in the Commons for a division, you really had little time to yourself simply to sit and brood, sit and read the papers? If it wasn't writing a speech, or checking a speech – a draft speech – or going to a meeting, there was some other thing that you had to do.

Yes, I think that's broadly true. I found it always desirable to try and fit in some time each week when I could talk to officials. When I was Parliamentary Secretary, I think I enjoyed a talk with Nenk more than anybody who you've mentioned. When I was Minister, I always tried 'no holds barred' discussions with senior officials – Mr Weaver, Mr Part and latterly Mr Rossetti, who came as Deputy Secretary in place of Part.* Can I just say one thing, slightly critical, looking back? How much weight you carry in the Cabinet on your own subject depends quite a bit on the amount of contribution you make, not only on your own subject, but on other subjects too. I don't think, looking back, I quite pulled my weight in Cabinet on general issues like the Common Market, and things like electoral strategy. One reason for this was that there weren't that many good all-rounders in the Department at briefing one, on general Cabinet issues. I make this point, not to be critical of the very gifted senior people at the Ministry, but because I'm not sure Departments realize how much they gain if they have an organized system for briefing Ministers on general Cabinet issues.

Isn't that really because of civil service structure? It would have to be a private Cabinet that would advise you on general policy.†

This is true up to a point. Indeed, I occasionally had that, too, in the form of successive very good Private Secretaries. They used to get some stuff for me by ringing up Whitehall to

*H. F. Rossetti was Deputy Under-Secretary of State for Education from 1963 to 1968.

†The system used in France when Ministers bring with them their personal advisers.

look it out for me. And I can remember ringing up people like Douglas Allen, who is now Permanent Secretary to the Treasury, to get material. But, nonetheless, one or two all-rounders in the Department on tap (this applied particularly, of course, to the Permanent Secretary himself, or herself) – this is an enormous help to oneself and to the Department as well. If you're the sort of person who has good points to make in Cabinet this will strengthen your weight with your colleagues generally. And looking back on it, Nenk of course was the sort of person with whom you could discuss almost anything, any major current issue, and he would have something rather interesting to say about it. He had just exactly that sort of gift I'm talking about. Derek Morrell, too.

You said before that such junior Ministers as Chris Chataway could and did take a fair amount of the work. What burdens could you place on such civil servants as your principal Private Secretary?

Well, one's principal Private Secretary is a crucial person in Ministerial life, whether junior or senior. If you're a junior Minister – I mean, I can remember well, Maurice, the way you fought my battles, not only battles in the Department, but also battles with Members' Private Secretaries. When you become a Minister the Principal Private Secretary is more important particularly with an outlying Department, like Education at Curzon Street. When you're dealing a lot of the time with local authorities, the links between your principal Private Secretary and Downing Street are essential to your efficiency and to keep you in touch with what's going on. Geoffrey Cockerill, who was my principal Private Secretary throughout 1963, he had a relationship with Philip Woodfield at Number Ten which was of enormous value. And if there is something troublesome – I'm not thinking just in terms of major policy – that comes up, a good understanding between your private office and Downing Street is just vital. But of course, there's much more to it. You travel around a lot with your principal Private Secretary. I can remember Dame Mary Smieton, who did take trouble about these sorts of personal matters, saying,

'You know, I do realize how essential it is that you should have somebody you find personally congenial, somebody you can share ideas with – this is essential.'* I was a strong supporter, as a member of the Fulton Committee, of our recommendation that it should be perfectly normal – no excitement caused – if an incoming Minister wants to change his incoming Private Secretary, and this should apply, in my view, to the Prime Minister too; I think he is absolutely entitled to choose who he wants as his principal Private Secretary. Happily, when the incoming Prime Minister this summer did change his principal Private Secretary, the press, I thought, were reasonably sensible about this – there was no tremendous excitement made and I'm quite certain there shouldn't be. And Alexander Isserlis made the same point very effectively himself in his own statement.†

Could I take up your description of Education as 'outlying'?

It's partly for reasons of finance – Education is spending a great deal of money, and it's bound to be unpopular with a number of people who don't quite understand the inwardness of maintained schools. And it's a combination with the fact that Curzon Street is geographically on its own; it's spiritually a bit on its own. Inevitably Curzon Street and the LEAS are closer with each other than either are with the rest of Whitehall. You've got to be a bit of an outsider in the government, a bit of a rogue elephant in the government, as Minister of Education. David Eccles performed this role exactly right, I think. It was harder to do it when you've come straight from the Treasury. I think, perhaps, I didn't make life easier for myself by having as my two chief interests economics and education, because that particular transition is not all that easy a one to make.

*Dame Mary Smieton was Permanent Secretary to the Ministry of Education, 1961–3.
†Alexander Isserlis, now an Under-Secretary in the Home Office, was Principal Private Secretary to Harold Wilson. Edward Heath decided not to appoint him as is the normal practice of a Minister coming into office. Isserlis took the unusual step of stating publicly that this decision was a perfectly proper one for a Minister to make.

Does what you have said about your relationship with your principal Private Secretary substantiate what you say about lack of conflict between civil servants and Ministers? A Private Secretary has to be completely loyal to the Minister and yet none whom we know ever has suffered through being loyal to their Minister even when it meant standing up to the Department.

Yes. I think you're quite right about that. Civil Servants never lose by being tough. What is wrong is perhaps the rare occasion – none in my time – when the principal Private Secretary gives himself the style of Minister and Permanent Secretary all in one. A principal Private Secretary, if he's worth his salt, can be totally loyal to his Minister, of enormous value to him, and yet never forget to slip in the thought that the Department is there. I must, though, mention one other function of a principal Private Secretary. I can think of other ones I've known, at the Treasury, for example, reminding one every now and then of who, a bit further down the line, is good. It isn't difficult for a Minister to suggest that A or B comes up to some meeting. I mean, if you suggested somebody from a completely irrelevant branch, that would be another matter, but it isn't difficult if you're having a discussion to say casually to the Permanent Secretary, 'I wonder whether Mr So-and-So mightn't attend this meeting as well,' and a wise Permanent Secretary will soon spot what's up and will say 'Yes'. And I've always been in favour of a bit of creative tension in government Departments as in university departments, and knowing who are the brighter sparks lower down the line. Of course, the Under-Secretary has a crucial position – he's the point at which administration and policy meet, but quite often people lower down, who have got ideas, are useful to bring up.

That answer disclaims the Minister's managerial role in his Department. You are saying the Minister asks a Permanent Secretary who might come to the meeting, and the way you have not put it is that 'I, as Minister, will determine who are the civil servants who will be at my meeting' – the civil servants are the Permanent Secretary's subordinates, rather than the Minister's?

Well, Maurice, I think one has got to be realistic here. I'm thinking of people whom I didn't see very often and whom I can't have known all that well and it seems to me just from the point of view of administrative style, if you like, a certain delicacy in talking to your most senior advisers is sensible. I think the style 'Don't you think it would be a good idea perhaps to have Mr So-and-So up for this discussion' is a more sensible way of proceeding than 'I want him to come'.

How far were major decisions that you had to make at the DES generated by you and your colleague Ministers? Weren't a large number of them already there for you – in the pipeline – to approve or turn down?

The pressure of numbers was one constant determiner of policies. Our decisions about higher education were shaped by the rapid growth of the sixth forms in the 1950s, and you cannot improve one part of the service without throwing up implications for the rest. There were some decisions less pressing and even optional. I'm thinking of the raising of the school-leaving age. In theory, we could have continued to stall on this but I didn't want to. And I was enormously helped in January 1964, after the publication of Newsom, by one member of the Cabinet (I won't mention him by name) who drafted a statement for the Cabinet in defence of stalling. The other members of the Cabinet had only to hear these words for this alternative to have no appeal whatever. It was rather interesting; they knew exactly what it would be like being a Minister of Education having to make that statement.

The Constraints on the Minister's Power: His Freedom of Action

What major limitations did you experience as Secretary of State for Education? How far were you a free agent? What limitations from within the government were placed on your authority by the Prime Minister, or the whole Cabinet, or the Treasury or, for that matter, other Ministers with competing interests for resources?

I think this is, in a way, the most important question you've put to me, because in so many books on politics people write about the Minister as though he took so many important decisions entirely by himself. Maybe, having been in Education, I overrate this point, but there are few important decisions that don't involve money. Much the biggest limitation on any Minister of Education is the need to get Treasury agreement, to get the resources he needs to implement policy. One curious change between 1962, say, and 1970 was in the doctrine enunciated by a very senior civil servant at the Treasury. The Treasury's line, and quite a plausible one from their point of view, had been restrictive on capital expenditure – partly because this is in the power of the government to control, in detail, and partly because every increase in capital expenditure generates increases in recurrent expenditure. Therefore, we had the biggest fight over the building programme. To be fair to the Treasury they tried to operate this policy a bit selectively. It was always easier to get a bit more on the building programme for further education than for other things because of the Treasury doctrine that this affected economic growth most. The last building programme I announced just before the 1964 Election was really quite generous. I think today the doctrine has changed a little – it seems to be easier for successive Ministers to get more money for school improvements and I think this is partly because the Treasury has now found the means of putting the recurrent bill more onto local authorities.* Whereas some years ago the emphasis was on whether central government oughtn't to take more of the education bill, the present line is to be very tough on the rate-support grant and therefore to put more pressure on local authorities. This will always be a bit attractive to governments, particularly if the political control locally tends to be the opposite to the political control at the centre.

One had to fight not only against the Treasury, but complete

*Presumably a reference to the ending of percentage grants (through which central government met a fixed proportion of local authority expenditure) and its substitution by general rate-support grants, which give a predetermined amount to local authorities, irrespective of the actual outlay of expenditure.

with other Ministers for resources. There was always, naturally, a tendency to say, 'Well now look, we can't let this Minister have a lot extra now, we must look at it all when it comes to the Public Investment Programme for the future.' There was always, equally, a tendency for the Treasury to say, 'Well, thank God, at any rate we've got Education screwed down a bit this year, even if we've had to give more for Housing, or something.' But one just had to be in on this one all the time – what I think are sometimes called 'salami' tactics are the only ones, as I see it, any Minister of Education can pursue. And just occasionally, if you battered away at a problem long enough, you got your way – as over teacher supply; this was something that caused great ill feeling between the Departments in 1961 and 1962, yet turned out to be a pushover in January 1963. I've always been grateful to Boyd-Carpenter for that ... just as I was grateful to him over his backing over Robbins and his backing over one Minister, rather than two.* But this was easily the biggest thing you had to fight and it wasn't even a question of shooting down the birds, it was also a question of retrieving them. Even when you felt you'd got your way over the school leaving age, you would often then have just as big a battle over the size of the programmes to be approved to implement the policy.

You've rightly picked out the important resource questions – when has the Treasury a determinant say? There are other issues such as selective versus non-selective education, the pattern of further and higher education, which aren't necessarily determined by financial or resource constraints. They are non-financial issues in education. To what extent is that sort of thing left to the Secretary of State? For example, would you have had to consult your colleagues on religious education or corporal punishment if these things had happened to come up?

Of course there's much less pressure to go to Cabinet when a thing doesn't involve another Department. I never put in – in

*John Boyd-Carpenter was at this time Chief Secretary to the Treasury; see also p. 106.

answer to your question, to the best of my recollection – a paper on selective versus non-selective education to the Cabinet because, although it was becoming an issue then, it was less so than it became afterwards and it didn't affect anybody else. I did put in a Shadow Cabinet paper in 1967 on that subject when it clearly had become a political issue, an issue within the party. Mr Heath's speech of the summer of 1967, in which he acknowledged the trend away from separate schools at eleven, considerably reflected the discussion we had on that paper. I think there was always less pressure on one to put in a paper on an issue that only affected one's own Department. In fact, your colleagues were a little apt to be cross if you bored them with a topic which was neither politically eye-catching, nor was something which any of the rest of them were involved with. A good example was the organization of higher education. Just before I became Minister of State I put in a paper to the relevant Cabinet Committee on this subject which, to some extent, pre-figured the debate we had in the House of Commons in March 1965 which Crosland and I opened. I looked up in the Cabinet Office that paper of mine and borrowed from it pretty considerably. I learned afterwards that Herbert Andrew, the Permanent Secretary, was heard to say to the Deputy Secretary, Mr Weaver, 'How did you manage to brief both front benches so well?' This is the explanation! But you weren't expected to put in Cabinet papers on things which weren't affecting other Departments and which didn't have much political mileage in them at that time.

What about other issues affecting machinery of government? Which Department should control higher education – the Treasury, or one education Ministry or two, for example?

That never went to Cabinet, because it involved Ministerial appointments, you see. Nothing goes to Cabinet which involves the Prime Minister making an appointment, and I can remember one Cabinet Minister, Geoffrey Rippon, saying, 'Look, really we must discuss this – I know this is a matter which involves appointments by the Prime Minister, but it is a policy issue also.'* One or two other Cabinet Ministers, I think, were a bit vexed that because of the Cabinet conventions we couldn't discuss what was clearly an important party decision – important politically, by the way, as well as educationally because it involved personal appointments. Can I just enlarge on this for a moment? I'm fascinated on reading my old press cuttings through (I've got twenty volumes of press cuttings in this Lodge from my Parliamentary career) to find that this issue of one Minister or two for higher education generated the most tremendous amount of press interest in the winter of 1963–4 and practically everybody, for a long time, seemed to assume that 'two Ministers' would win. This was one of those occasions when 'informed comment' actually showed itself rather ill-informed because I think it was in fact very unlikely that the case for two Ministers should ever have been won. The Prime Minister was new to being Prime Minister and inclined, I think, to the one-Minister solution. You had the Treasury, which was then the sponsoring Department for the machinery of government, very much inclined to the one-Minister solution – always had been, and Boyd-Carpenter himself and his advisers were very much on this side. As people will remember, the one public controversy about this took place at the Ministry, not so much between Quintin Hogg and myself as between Boyd-Carpenter and Hogg – there was really a rather hilarious confrontation at Curzon Street in front of the educational press.† In fact, the outcome of this was we had a single Secretary of State, and the single Secretary of State was Mr Hogg – that was always, I think, the predictable outcome – but what finally decided it, and I think there's no difficulty about making this public now, was the debate in the House of Lords when everybody agreed that Lord James beat Lord Robbins in argument on this subject.‡ Everybody

*Geoffrey Rippon has been the Minister responsible for Common Market negotiations since November 1970. At that time (1962 to 1964) he was Minister of Public Building and Works. He joined the Cabinet in 1963.

†John Boyd-Carpenter was also representing the Treasury as the Department then responsible for universities. He was then Chief Secretary to the Treasury.

‡Lord James was at this time Vice-Chancellor. University of York.

agreed that the case for a single Secretary of State had been made. It was also pretty obvious, from a speech by my own predecessor here at Leeds, Sir Roger Stevens, at his first Court meeting – and Sir Roger showed great courage in coming into the open about this at his very first Court meeting – and from Lord James's speech in the House of Lords, that the university world wasn't united behind two Ministers,* whereas the rest of the educational world *was* absolutely united behind the idea of a single Secretary of State. If by any chance the decision for two Ministers had gone that way, I couldn't, I think, have stayed on in the government. I think my position with the educational world would have been impossible – I never threatened resignation, but I'd always decided in my own mind. I couldn't have stayed on. But I equally made it plain to Selwyn Lloyd, among other people, before Christmas, that if Alec Home was ready to go for a single Secretary of State I didn't in the least mind who that was – in fact I was quite ready to give up being a member of the Cabinet if that made it easier, though in fact nobody wanted me to do that.† But this was an interesting case of really rather an important policy decision which never came up to the Cabinet because it was regarded as a matter strictly within the Prime Minister's own personal province and the press forecast it wrongly. The Robbins case wasn't well argued and thank goodness Mr Shearman put in that minority vote of dissent.‡ What seems now to be rather ironic and sad is that now we have one Secretary of State we are in danger of splitting into two Departments again. There is a real risk of a situation developing in which the UGC is regarded as the sponsoring Department for the universities and where the DES looks like the sponsoring

*Sir Roger Stevens was Vice-Chancellor, University of Leeds, 1963–70. He was formerly Deputy Under-Secretary of State, Foreign Office, and adviser to the First Secretary of State on Central Africa.

†At that time Selwyn Lloyd was Lord Privy Seal and Leader of the House of Commons. He is now Speaker of the House of Commons. Sir Alec Douglas-Home was Prime Minister October 1963–October 1964 and has been Foreign Secretary since June 1970.

‡Harold Shearman argued in a minority report against the majority view that there should be separate ministries for higher and 'lower' education. He was a member of the Robbins Committee and Chairman of the London Education Committee.

Department for the polytechnics. That, I think, would be a sad outcome.

The assumption that decisions about machinery of government aren't connected with the policies that the machinery exists to pursue seems nonsensical. More generally, can a Minister decide what goes to Cabinet?

Every now and then there's a protest about the number of things going to the Cabinet – protests from other Ministers who say small matters of expenditure shouldn't be allowed to go to Cabinet. On the other hand, I think it's pretty difficult to deny a Minister a right to take a decision which is important to him politically and which may be important to the government. It's a matter for your private office to negotiate with the Cabinet office about this – the Cabinet Secretary, Sir Burke Trend, consults the Prime Minister about what goes on the agenda but you don't get turned down if you've got any sort of case – you may be asked, 'Are you really going to push the case this far?'*

Are there some matters which, by form, go to the Cabinet? Foreign affairs every week, for example?

Yes, though foreign affairs statements can be the least invigorating part of Cabinet business. This is the sort of thing that always makes me think how careful one's got to be when writing history not to attach too much significance to chance remarks, and indeed the best historians know this. Do you remember the story in G. M. Young of Baldwin saying when foreign affairs were being discussed: 'Wake me up when you are finished with that,' and this has always been cited as an example of Baldwin's lack of interest in foreign affairs.† But gracious me. I can think of statements I've heard on foreign affairs that could well have prompted the same reaction, and it's very seldom one has a really good foreign affairs debate in the Cabinet.

*Secretary to the Cabinet since 1963.
†G. M. Young, *Stanley Baldwin*, Rupert Hart-Davis, 1952, p. 63. Young attributes this not so much to lack of interest as being 'outside the range of Baldwin's natural intelligence'.

Is the Cabinet concerned more with short-term crises in the economy or foreign affairs than with the long-term future of British society – the future of education, health, and the other social services?

I think one might put it even more strongly than that. The Cabinet increasingly, as the years go on, tends to be most concerned with the agenda that the press and media are setting out as the crucial issues before the nation at any one time. Now if education at any moment figures on that agenda it probably will come before Cabinet. There are, of course, decisions about public expenditure to be taken all the time, but I would say that any Minister who tried to get real interest in something that didn't involve a decision on expenditure was a long-term issue but not one on the accepted agenda, would be more likely to meet bored acquiescence from his colleagues, rather than active agreement. It is one of the things that worries me about TV – it isn't so much that TV shapes the answers but it shapes the agenda too much. If something is identified by one of the leading interviewers as a crucial point on which to question the parties on their policies, it's thought by the public that this is one of the vital issues. It is not easy for a Minister to say 'Look we oughtn't to be so concerned as we are at this minute about A and B and C to the exclusion of all else; really what I'm saying about J is just as important'.

So issues that reach the Cabinet are important but not the sole indicators of what is important.

Can I just add one topical supplement to my last answer? I think the issue of student dissent, student militancy, its genesis, how it comes to be, what our attitude ought to be to it – I think this is an important fact about university policy at the present time. I most emphatically don't think it's the single most important aspect of university policy and to create excitement either way about a decision to open a second bank account in a university is to get matters fantastically out of perspective.* However, when I go to London the first thing

*A reference to student protest against some universities' patronage of banks which have business connections in South Africa.

people want to speak to me about is 'What are the students like?' 'How are they behaving?' and it's no good my getting impatient and saying, 'We oughtn't to be going on about these students all the time, there are many other matters in university just as important' – people would merely think I was evading the issue. I always become annoyed when people insist the conventionally accepted priorities must be right, rather than my own. The analogy is when the government at any moment has apparently got to conform to what is the nationally accepted agenda. Now, your second question about the Cabinet. The Cabinet is the nearest approach we have in this country, I think, to a completely sovereign body. It isn't totally sovereign in that the balance of payments, as Christopher Dow* used to say, is a restraint on all our other activities. The Cabinet is considerably and increasingly affected by what it's expected to do, I think. But it is, nonetheless, the chief expression of the fact that the major political differences in our national life are not so much between government and opposition as between the government and everybody else. Governments 'do', the rest of us talk. This is close to a hobbyhorse of mine. I agree with Macmillan in regretting this jargon about 'Shadow Ministers' which I think only confuses the issue. A Minister is a Minister and a Shadow Minister isn't. Even 'Shadow Cabinet' ought, ideally, to appear in quotes and when I was once even described as 'Minister of Education in the Shadow Cabinet' I protested vigorously! But it was no good, you see. It was just like what I was saying about the students, because public opinion had accepted that there were 'Shadow Ministers', it really wasn't any good pointing that out. This is a worrying thing about British politics – the small extent to which we are prepared to listen to those who question the conventional wisdom, whether it's about the agenda or the terms we use.

However, what you say does really throw doubt on Haldane's description of the Cabinet as the mainspring of all the mechan-

*Christopher Dow has been Assistant Secretary-General, O E C D since 1963. He served in the Treasury as Economic Adviser, 1945–54, and again as Senior Economic Adviser, 1962–3.

ism of government.* It's obviously the most important point of convergence, but the mainsprings of activity really are elsewhere in the system?

Yes – except that a Cabinet decision is rightly regarded with particular respect by everybody in the government machine. There's a terrible story – but it is, in fact, quite true – about a former Home Secretary who was seeing a deputation and started to utter a slightly loose sentence in the course of his remarks, and his extremely authoritarian and bossy Permanent Secretary sharply interrupted and said, 'You can't say that, Home Secretary, you're talking about a Cabinet decision.' I think that was an intolerable thing to say in front of a deputation and would be said by very few Permanent Secretaries today, but nonetheless, it wasn't technically out of line.† They are the most important directives of all that Permanent Secretaries ever get. If ever there has been important discussion in Cabinet the Permanent Secretary or his office will probably ring up before even the Minister gets back to find out how it went and what conclusions were reached. The importance of the drafting of Cabinet conclusions cannot be overrated. The Secretaries to the Cabinet do this very well. Curiously enough the Cabinet conclusion on the raising of the school-leaving age at the end of January 1964 was worded in a way that was just slightly ambiguous and gave the Treasury some handle for saying that we hadn't reached the conclusion that everybody else thought we had. I definitely thought it had been agreed that we should plan on the assumption that the school-leaving age would be raised in the year 1970–71, but the wording was just ambiguous. When I rang up Sir Burke Trend he said to me, 'Yes, my understanding of the discussion and the conclusion reached is just the same as yours, any difference about this is purely verbal, and please quote me, if it helps you, as endorsing your understanding of what was decided.' It certainly isn't my experience that Secretaries to the Cabinet abuse this power. They are very reasonable if you have occasion,

*See p. 37.
†In one sense it was 'out of line'. In strict Parliamentary theory, Ministers are individually accountable to Parliament and not to the Cabinet.

with a good case, to seek clarification, about just what was decided. Somebody opening those minutes may quite possibly attribute significance to a conclusion which it really wasn't intended to have at the time. I so often say to myself, when I read of a report of some significant historical discovery in newly opened archives, 'I wonder if this is just what those details at that time precisely *meant*.'

We've talked about the relationships with the Prime Minister and about the relationships between the Ministers and Cabinet. What about other parts of the inter-Departmental machinery? What about the role of the Treasury, for example? You saw it from both sides as a Treasury Minister and as Education Minister. What was their role in the creating or restraining of the pursuit of educational objectives? Did they simply collate the policy impetuses from the different Departments, or did they themselves express a view of educational and other objectives more positively?

Really the Treasury came into this in three ways. There was, first of all, their overriding concern about the rate of increase of government expenditure, which expressed itself most, of course, in the concern about the improvement element in the educational programme. Nobody doubted that when you had more at school, schooling was going to cost more, but there was the question about how much the improvement element should be. Again, just what was a reasonable rate of increase per year in expenditure on further education? This, of course, was one of the biggest factors during my years as Minister. The arguments used to be between whether you took a 10 per cent (in real terms) increase, or $12\frac{1}{2}$ per cent – as big as that. Thirdly, there is always the propensity of the Treasury to think of itself not only as the best Department, but as the Department which really knows other Departments' work better than they do themselves. I think that, in the old days when the Treasury was the Ministry of Economic Affairs, the Ministry of Finance and the Civil Service Department all rolled into one, there was always the tendency for the Treasury to become the overlord. Certainly, the Treasury was not above this when it came to dealing with education. I'm saying this, having had experience from both ends. Just occasionally I would find myself saying, as Financial Secretary, 'But I don't think this is quite the point the Ministry of Education's on.' Though there were other times when the Treasury were, I think, more reasonable in raising an issue. For example, the Treasury, I think with a bit of justice in 1961, said, 'Well, if we agree that the CATs should go "direct grant" do let us be quite clear this is ultimately, here and now, prejudging the issue, whether the CATs become universities or not.'

That delineates one Treasury role – the staff role, the financial Departmental role, of pointing out that there are going to be further consequences of present educational policies, which will then have financial implications. They weren't saying, 'This is a bad educational policy' or 'good educational policy'. They were saying, 'You educational policy makers must be clear, in the first place, about your own policy implications, and secondly about the financial consequences of the policy.'

They were saying exactly what you put first, Maurice. I think this was an attitude that one couldn't criticize. 'This decision is going to have educational consequences, in terms of what's going to happen after Robbins, and that again, in its turn, will breed financial consequences.' There was no attempt on this subject to argue the educational case – what's this going to mean for other technical colleges in years to come? I have always had in my mind that little episode, because it caused quite sharp discussion for a time, as the most justified example of the Treasury intervening to point out the implications of an educational decision.

The Department looked on CATs going 'direct grant' as simply the fulfilment of the 1956 White Paper.* It's the common situation when you're looking at two different models – you're looking through two different perspectives. That de-

*The colleges of advanced technology were maintained by local education authorities, until Eccles decided to make them independent institutions receiving direct grants from the Ministry.

cision for the CATs was rather like the Robbins recommendation on the training colleges. I've always had a certain sympathy for the colleges about this. When you think how rapidly the CATs were designated and got to direct grant status and then to university status, it's hard not to feel that the colleges of education have had a much, much longer and much tougher row to hoe.

The third way in which the Treasury came into education was, or course, that it was the sponsoring department for the universities until 1963. And that situation, everyone agreed, had to go. Whatever else happened after Robbins, whether we had one Minister or two, the one certain thing was that it was wrong for the Treasury, which was the department concerned with controlling public expenditure, to be a spending Department.

Could we discuss the more general question about the way in which the government machine formulates objectives within the Departments and reconciles objectives as between the different Departments? Was the Ministry, during your time as a Minister, formulating its objectives? What was the machinery for formulating long-term objectives?

We didn't have a planning branch of course, at that time.* As a member of the Fulton Committee I was rather in favour of the Minister having a Chief Policy Adviser, something a bit more akin to the economic section of the Treasury.† (I was thinking how it worked under Sir Robert Hall).‡ This was not one of the more popular recommendations and it was rather unpopular with some members of the 'Shadow Cabinet', incidentally, who said this ought to be very much a matter of individual ministerial style.** But others on the Fulton

*See pp. 31 and 183.

†The report of the Fulton Committee, *The Civil Service* (*Fulton Report*) (H M S O, 1968) recommended that each Department should have a Chief Policy Adviser reporting directly to the Minister.

‡Sir Robert Hall was Economic Adviser to the government from 1953 to 1961.

**The stronger objection would be the artificial division between 'policy' and its administration, which was to rest with the Permanent Secretary, to whom the Chief Policy Adviser would not be accountable.

Committee, besides myself, saw the advantages of a Chief Policy Advisor who would have more time than the Permanent Secretary to identify, and work on, longer-term issues. Just occasionally this was done well and rigorously in the Department. For example, I saw the planning paper that led up to the creation of the Curriculum Study Group and that was a lengthy but rigorous piece of work – a real attempt at doing just what you say.* I don't recall over secondary reorganization we ever did this – in fact there were those in the Department who identified the issue quite wrongly and there were those, even high up, who were inclined to say, 'How can we do away with the 11-plus examination?' without realizing it was separate schools at the moment of transfer from primary to secondary which was the point at issue. I think one reason for that was the sensitivity Departments always have about putting up any paper which involves something they feel will be politically quite out of the question with the government concerned. Now, you may well say the Departments are too apt to do Ministers' political thinking for them – I think they are. But, nonetheless, I can understand the sort of feeling in the Department at that period. Defending the top grammar schools in their existing form seemed an absolute 'must' for the government at that time and therefore to put up anything which cast doubt on that was sort of going beyond their proper function. But it would have been acceptable, and useful, if somebody had put up a paper saying, in effect, that we all realize the importance which many people, including many government supporters, do attach to the continuation of some of the finest grammar schools, but nonetheless, the trend of opinion is increasingly moving away from segregation at the age of eleven. Might it not be a good idea to consider two things? First of all, not just tolerating, but positively encouraging comprehensive schooling and going out for it in the areas where it clearly makes sense. Instead of saying, 'Yes, it's all right to try experiments with comprehensive schools in new housing estates in rural areas,' say rather more positively, 'This is what we expect in the growing housing areas, particularly in the country districts, we expect this to happen increasingly.' I think one

*See p. 170.

mistake, Maurice, at the time when you and I were together, was the way the Ministry sanctioned those dribs and drabs of two-form-entry secondary schools in the late 1950s. If the Ministry had said to Ministers, 'Let's try and run this so that we don't have too many small secondary schools which could easily complicate decisions for the future,' I believe Ministers would have taken that. I think there were certain ways in which a planning paper could have effected a change in policy at that time without setting opinion – even Conservative opinion – by the ears. So on some issues the planning and formulation of objectives were done well, sometimes not so well, and I think there was more to be said for the Fulton recommendations than people sometimes think.

You quote Eccles as saying that in the early 1970s educational expenditure was going to be vastly greater than anything contemplated at that time, that the system was going to expand. You have also said that one part of the system is dependent on the other, that you can't change one bit without changing other bits of it. All of this would argue for a good 'objectives game' within the planning machinery of the Department – taking stock of what development in secondary education, FE, universities and elsewhere might mean in terms of declared objectives and in the relationship between different or perhaps conflicting objectives. In fact, the examples you've quoted have been of single-policy strands that might have been done well, or badly. This isn't quite playing the 'objectives game' in the way that the Swedes or the French or the Dutch have in their indicative planning. Am I right in thinking that the system in your time, and for that matter, since your time, has never grasped the importance of getting out all of the objectives at once, testing them as to feasibility as well as to policy desirability? It would surely not be politically difficult to do this?

That's quite right and, of course, one reason for that is that people didn't see, or very few of us did, at the turn of the 1950s and 1960s the scale of what was happening. The implications of the pressure of numbers in the sixth forms in the 1950s, higher education and advanced further education in the 1960s – one had some glimmering of it but, looking back now, I wish when I had become Minister I had put in hand a real exercise in indicative planning. Assuming certain limitations from the point of view of resources, what was the best 'mix' to go for. I remember Chris Chataway saying this to me and he was quite right. One ought to have asked, 'Now, assuming, say 5 per cent a year in real terms more for the education service, what are the alternative models of what we could get for that?'

Another reason why I think what you have said is both right and important is that officials are sometimes too nervous of carrying out a rigorous examination of policy in what are felt to be 'politically sensitive' areas. Obviously no civil servant would ever be so silly as to suggest to a Conservative government that, for instance, the scope of public enterprise should be widened. But I think that, looking back, because of the political and educational significance of the most prestigious grammar schools to a Conservative government, there was rather too much inhibition against carrying out any policy planning where secondary-school reorganization was concerned, and also against recognizing the implications of the fact that selection at 11-plus was already on the defensive.

You said Education has always seemed to be a bit separate from the rest of Whitehall. Does this denote the value placed on education and social policy generally within different governments? Those who come up through social service Departments as civil servants on the whole stand a less good chance of getting to the top of the civil service, for example. And the same is true of Ministers.* Is education regarded as a humdrum, less glamorous, less important part of government activity?

This is difficult. It is true that the key Ministers in a government, besides the Prime Minister, are the Chancellor of the Exchequer, the Foreign Secretary, and the Secretary of State for Defence. The head of the new Health and Social Services

*See p. 62, n. 27.

Department is a job of considerable importance. And, of course, Ministers know and feel that education is important. Reggie Maudling used often to talk to me about education as investment. He had, always, a rather acutely sceptical critical approach to this – not so much disbelieving as wishing he understood it better. What I think is true is that few other members of the Cabinet who haven't been there understand the inwardness of the educational world. The inwardness of the world of the maintained schools, and the inwardness even of things like secondary reorganization. How few people do until you force them to it. There were some happy exceptions in the Conservative Research Department, for instance Tony Greenland, who briefed one quite admirably. He realized that the alternatives are not either grammar schools and modern schools on the one side, or allthrough comprehensives, purpose-built or 'botched up' on the other. How few people really understand about two-tier and three-tier schemes.

The same could be said for many ordinary backbench MPs who would not understand more than a half of the papers that go up to Treasury Ministers – this doesn't detract from the glamour of the Treasury or the importance attributed to it. All things are technical. I have, at the back of my mind, the fact that the most two recent Swedish Prime Ministers were Ministers of Education. Somehow this couldn't happen here . . .?

You're quite right if you think of the people since the war who have been most associated with Education. It isn't a Department which has enhanced one's career in politics.

There was a remarkable change and it came, I think, with your tenure. Before you came the Department of Education was a sort of ante-room which was either for people who were passing through on their way up, or for people passing through on their way down.

David Eccles, clearly, was a key minister. Eccles made it a more purposive Department than ever before and he was glad enough to get back to it in 1959 from the Board of Trade.

What impact do MPs have on educational policy making?

Well there are two questions here. This is more important than some people think. I think Parliament is a rather more important partner to the education service than it always gets the credit for being. Some forty or fifty MPs, in all parties added together, follow education and take an active part in the debates. It's very much level pegging these days between the two sides, much more so than fifteen years ago, and whether they like to admit it or not, they have more in common with one another than with the rest of the House of Commons. They do understand the inwardness, they talk the same kind of language. If they sometimes express what may seem rather extreme views, like Christopher Price or Stan Newens,* well this all comes out 'in the wash'. In the debate, of course, you have some members going out on a limb in some directions, some in others, but there's no doubt that MPs reflect pretty well all those who follow education. It is not difficult to detect the general sort of state of doctrine on most educational subjects. If one looked at the Vote of Censure at the beginning of this Parliament on Mrs Thatcher about secondary reorganization, some of the speeches made on the Conservative side, by people like Charlie Morrison, and the excellent maiden speech by Tim Raison, accurately registered the change in the norm of thinking on this during the last four or five years.† Now in addition to the Members who take an active part in debate, there is also the 1922 Committee‡ and the Party Committee. Just as with the Party Conference, I felt with the 1922 Committee that I was winning over a bit more support, or neutralizing a bit more opposition, each time I spoke to them. I'm thinking particularly of secondary reorganization, and as more Members, county or city, started reorganizing, I felt that I was carrying a little bit more of opinion with me.

*Christopher Price was Labour MP for Perry Barr (until 1970) and Parliamentary Private Secretary to Anthony Crosland (see p. 165). He is also Education Correspondent of the *New Statesman*. Stan Newens was Labour MP for Epping, 1964–70. He was a member of the *Tribune* group of MPs.

†Charles Morrison has been MP for Devizes since 1964, and is Chairman of the Wiltshire Education Committee.

‡A committee of all Conservative back-benchers.

Incidentally, I would like to give the lie direct to Andrew Alexander's assertion in his book on the 1970 election that 90 per cent of the party were against me on this subject.* I don't think it was true in 1968, which was the period about which he was writing, and it certainly wasn't true in 1969. It might conceivably have been true of 90 per cent of those Tory members whom he himself spoke to most often but it certainly wasn't true of 90 per cent of the whole party.

So MPs are an important part of the power structure part of the political environment in which Ministers have got to move, and got to be reconciled with. But the actual creation of policy is not with MPs.

No, but they are a very important occasion for registering the norm of thinking and how it is changing. Can I just add one other thing about MPs? Nothing is more important, if you're a Minister or an opposition spokesman, than seeing your Party Committee has a Whip who is objective and records the proceedings of your Party Committee fairly. Distorted reports from Whips cause more trouble to Parliamentary life and to Ministers than almost anything else.

You say that MPs have got this important role in enabling Ministers to test policy, to express the prevailing norms about education, but no large number, at least to judge from the attendance at debates, are interested in education. And is this not true of both parties, as compared with Economics, or Defence or Foreign Affairs?

I'm not quite with you on this one. Parliamentary debates as a whole are poorly attended these days. Winding-up speeches compared with twenty years back, are poorly attended. Yet I would say that both the numbers and the quality of members attending education debates are notably higher than they were fifteen years ago. In the early 1950s if you had a particular issue like Church schools, the Roman Catholic lobby – might encourage members to speak, but the number of MPs

*A. Alexander and A. Watkins, *The Making of a Prime Minister*, Macdonald, 1970.

who really follow education now and have an informed view of it is not so few, I think we've got the opposite problem now: Members sometimes thinking they have a better understanding of these issues than is really the case. I thought the Select Committee report on student relations was an unfortunate affair because it plunged rather wildly, rather unselfcritically, into tricky areas.* To give you an instance of a debate which was surprisingly well attended, the last set of Regulations on Teacher Training was debated on a morning sitting – one of the Crossman morning sittings – on a hot day, and it was quite surprising to see the numbers of members who turned up at 11 o'clock to talk about teacher training and the new regulations.† Many members do have a real conscience about this, they do feel even more than with the polytechnics that the colleges of education have rather the bad end of the stick, at the moment.

In local government, is education probably the single largest issue?

You're quite right. It's a more sought-after committee in local government than it is in Parliament. It's *the* committee, the general purposes sub-committee of the education committee is tremendously popular – a thing many people seek to join. I have often been struck by the extraordinary contrast between those cities and counties where education policy is conducted broadly on a basis of concensus, and those cities where there has been strong party fighting. You get the first kind of atmosphere in Kent and Sussex, say, or the West Riding of Yorkshire where Alderman Broughton and Mrs Fitzpatrick really did pursue continuity. Not only did Mrs Fitzpatrick pursue a middle-of-the-road policy on comprehensive schools, but Broughton was very critical – indeed most courageously critical – of his own party and government over the cuts after devaluation. On the whole the cities, with some notable excep-

*Select Committee on Education and Science, *Report on Student Relations*, H C 449 of 1968–9.

†As Leader of the House of Commons, Richard Crossman introduced morning sittings of the whole House.

tions of which Leeds is one, have had a tradition of much more partisan fighting over this – I am inevitably thinking here of Birmingham and there is a vast difference here between Birmingham and Leeds or Bristol. But perhaps my views are coloured too much by my association with Birmingham, which was exceptionally severe in this respect. If one takes London throughout the whole period of Conservative opposition between 1964 and 1970 there was no more creditable moment than the decision to put Chris Chataway in charge of London's affairs in 1967. It was not my decision, obviously, it was the decision of Desmond Plummer,* of Willie Whitelaw, of Edward du Cann, of just everybody – that we must put the best person possible in charge, and I hope this was the Tory Party at its best. When a real emergency like this arises, we do try and get the best person for the job.

Could we just signal that important point you have made – in fact, the decision to make someone leader or the Chairman of the Education Committee, was not only a decision of the leader of the G L C but the Parliamentary chiefs also had a voice in this. Local authority appointments of this kind are subject to decision, not only by the local authority party chiefs, but also by the national ones?

And the party chiefs all routing the same direction about both whom they didn't want and whom they did want. This was only because it was London. It wouldn't have happened in Birmingham or Bristol.

After all, this was quite a moment – winning control of London for the first time for thirty-three years and actually winning control of inner London for the first time in thirty-three years. Some people felt this might be the one and only time. And there was a strong feeling that if by any incredible chance we won inner London, the party must have the best person possible, 'and this couldn't be just treated as one local decision among many. And I think that in this sort of situation the Conservative party does show itself up in its best light.'

The Labour Party never could do this. Could we now look

*Desmond Plummer is Leader of the Greater London Council.

at the Department itself? Would you care to describe how priorities are decided within the Department?

Yes, I must say, in my time there was not much central direction about this. A certain amount of in-fighting near the top went on – I'm not sure this was wholly a bad thing – but as I've said, I was to blame for not saying as Chris Chataway would have liked me to do, 'Let's have a plan – almost a George Brown type of exercise, over a limited field to ask ourselves what's the best we could get for 5 per cent a year extra.'* But certainly I would say there were the two traditions in the Department: the social justice tradition, wanting to widen opportunity, giving people the greater opportunity to acquire intelligence, and the technical college tradition – education for investment, education for efficiency. They were described in the early 1960s, rather happily I thought, by Toby Weaver, as 'the dialectic within the office' – and that dialectic was quite sharp.† Twenty years earlier the dialectic would have been thought inappropriate to the Board of Education anyway. But in fact, of course, the important thing is, who won here? What really won was the pressure of numbers, which made it essential to expand rapidly both FE and higher education; and the truest single phrase about education in the 1960s was spoken by David Watt in the *Financial Times*, at the appearance of one of the *Black Papers*, when he said, 'They don't seem to realize that "more" has come to stay.'‡

The machinery for determining priorities was simply that of having to send in estimates each year and later on estimates for PESC exercises and the rest.** These were then mediated by the Accountant-General's department before getting to Ministers for determination, carrying with them the historic commitments rather than an assessment of priorities according to newly revised objectives?§

*A reference to 'The National Plan', Cmnd. 2764, September 1965.
†See p. 24.   ‡See p. 60, n. 1.
**The Treasury's Public Estimates Survey Committee.
§The Accountant-General's department is the DES Finance Branch. The Under-Secretary in charge of finance is traditionally called the Accountant-General. He is not to be confused with the Accounting Officer who is the Permanent Secretary.

The importance of the Accountant-General in the Department was great here – always. Nenk as Accountant-General, we've already mentioned, was one of the outstanding creative thinkers, very tough minded, very hard headed, no sentimentalist, though socially extremely committed. I've also alluded to a later Accountant-General, Embling, to whom I would give very high marks as well.* And one thing that he did was to put our point of view most effectively to the Treasury, and the Treasury's point of view to us. He was good indeed at reminding us of just how tiresome we seemed to the Treasury from time to time, but it didn't alter the fact that when he was on the phone with the Treasury he got us the very best terms that he ever could . . . you know: 'Now you don't expect me to swallow that one?' He was absolutely as tough with them as he could be and very much respected in the Treasury. In fact a senior official remarked to me how fortunate we were to have him, especially during a period of major expenditure decisions, such as the expansion of teacher training, and the consequences of Robbins.

Some Ministers, including yourself, have referred to the government of education as a partnership between the Department, the local authorities and the teachers. Is this a really meaningful formulation of the relationship or is there any sense of the Secretary of State being the head of something that one can describe as a single managerial system, with authority and accountability running through it from head teacher of a school to the Secretary of State?

I think this is the hardest question you're putting to me. First of all, Maurice, there can't be a straight, single control here for the very simple reason that the Ministry directly controls so very little money. I mean most of the government money reaches local authorities through the rate-support grant now, which technically is not on the Ministry's vote at all, and it isn't the Minister who pays the teachers, for example – people often think it is.† On some matters, full-time maintenance grants

*See p. 73.

†Rate-support grant is paid by the Department for the Environment. The teachers are paid by local authorities under the Local Government Acts.

for students, for example, I know that the local authorities have
no option. Nonetheless, the fact that the Minister doesn't pay
for education directly, except for a small part of the service
and even then indirectly through the Department of the Environment, makes the idea of this being a centrally run service, like the Health Service, in my view, impossible. I still
think there is room for this concept of partnership. Now it's
true that the central government exercises a number of controls of which the most important, perhaps, is control over
capital investment. Nor can any school be started, no school
can be improved, or its status altered, without the Minister
giving his approval.* Equally, of course, as the law now stands,
the Minister can't compel an authority to reorganize an existing secondary school if it doesn't want to. The size of the rate-
support grant, though this doesn't come directly from the
Department of Education, helps determine what the local
authorities can do, what resources they'll have available. On
the other side I'd say three things that sometimes get left out.
The first is that quite a lot of important ideas in education
have come up from the local authorities and haven't all come
down from the Ministry – this was true in the old days, things
like Loughborough College, which was started originally with
no grant at all, which afterwards became the first CAT and
then the first technological university. The Leicestershire
scheme†, the first reorganization scheme, which did not involve
all-through comprehensives but did away with the 11-plus, that
was a local initiative. One of the strengths of the movement
behind local or secondary reorganization were initiatives coming from local authorities themselves. One of the reasons I've
never been for compulsion is because I believe you are going
to get better results in the long run if a general indication of
policy from the Minister is accompanied by local expression
of initiatives, rather than too many letters going out from the

*Control over capital investment is mediated through the Department's
building programme. This is separate from the Department's control over
the creation, closure or change of size or function of a school, which is a
quasi-judicial process under Section 13 of the Education Act, 1944.

†Leicestershire was the first authority to create comprehensive education by
establishing upper schools for pupils from fourteen onwards. This was begun
in 1957.

Department beginning, 'It is the Minister's intention. . . . It is the government's policy.' But if you're going to have selective intervention by the government, if you're going to have partnership, the sort of relationship I would like to see between the government and the local authorities, then this is certainly going to mean more civil servants. One of the things my old colleagues seem to me a bit woolly about is that they talk about fewer civil servants, yet they are deliberately pursuing policies – of which I don't necessarily disapprove – which must mean more civil servants. But there must be the right style of correspondence between civil servants and local bodies. I'm in favour of a partnership, of a sense of mutual involvement, and recognizing that you don't get social progress by compelling too many people to do what they don't want to do. There is a real difference between schools in certain parts of the country, and in the assumptions made about education. If I were talking about moral or religious education I wouldn't put it the same in Yorkshire as if I were talking in Surrey. The biggest force leading us away from partnership is the belief – in my view mistaken – that in the upshot nothing really matters or ought to matter except the policy of the central government. In Britain over the last ten or fifteen years, we've accompanied some mistrust of politics with an ever stronger belief that government policy matters supremely. Of course, on a number of important issues governments ought to choose. They ought to express their point of view – I've never concealed mine that in secondary education the educational arguments against early segregation are good arguments. But despite all this I would like to keep this concept of partnership going quite a bit longer.

Is this saying that on matters of overall structure, the system within which strategic policies are laid down, in matters on which there must be one law for the whole country, the age of entry and the school-leaving age for example, the centre will lay down policy, but that the style of education and the content of education are best developed at discretion by the local education authorities? The 'open' British primary school – now thought of as a model in the USA – came from Oxfordshire, Bristol, Leicestershire, West Riding. The best developments in school building probably came from Hertfordshire before they became part of nationally available (though not prescribed) design models. At the same time might there not be one system with very wide degrees of discretion in the 169 local authorities, with 169 policies, and in the 30,000 or so institutions that make up the primary and secondary schools?

Let me follow this point through by referring to secondary schools. You talk about 169 policies – I don't think we're going to have anything like that – but I do think that Southampton genuinely believes that the particular pattern they've got in Southampton – twelve to sixteen schools, followed by sixth-form colleges – is best for them. Leicestershire equally strongly believes in schools for ten to fourteen year olds, then fourteen onwards. The Isle of Wight, for their part, think they've been right to go for schools for children from nine to thirteen years, and that they should transfer at thirteen to upper schools. Now, it may be that pressure of public opinion is going to force greater uniformity here over the years. I see some real difficulty in, not so much people going from 11-plus authorities to areas of all-through comprehensives, as in movement between authorities which have quite different ages of transfer. I would like, for a good many years, to let Southampton, the Isle of Wight and Leicestershire try out their schemes, because we need experience before trying to lay down too much uniformity. Public opinion may not like this, but we just don't know enough for a government to be justified in describing any particular pattern of organization as *the* right one.

So catholicity in the system provides for experiment and innovation by strong local authority units. That catholicity is, however, reconcilable with central government policy making about the whole framework of education; in fact, that surely is the nature of indicative planning?

Yes, there is and has to be some central framework, I agree. But I'd hope that governments for the most part can play along with what local authorities genuinely want to do, rather than to have to impose too many things on them they don't want to do. I shall be very sorry if continuing disputes over Maud* and over local government reorganization mean that we have to go along with 169 local authorities for a great deal longer.

Could we now talk a bit about the relationship between the Department and the universities?

This rather bothers me. I thought the strongest argument for a single Secretary of State back in 1963 was that you really couldn't divide responsibility for higher education. And there's no doubt that that was the argument that weighed strongest with the government of the day.† There's no easy solution to this problem of the binary system.‡ I feel that out-and-out critics of the system tend to overlook two key points. Firstly, how much research should be undertaken in poly-technics and colleges of education, and of what kinds? It couldn't be sensible to try to replicate research which is already being undertaken in universities. Secondly, how much are we prepared to spend on building up the libraries of what are called the 'non-autonomous' institutions, so that they approxi-mate to university standards? It's no use shirking such ques-tions. But I agree that the binary system, as we have it today, is inherently unstable. I think what is going to happen – at Leeds, for example – is not a grand design for erasing all the lines straight away, but nonetheless, there are going to be close relationships between certain departments in the university and certain departments in the polytechnic. I think a policy of the Department saying to the polytechnics, 'Whatever you do, we must build you up and you must keep your distance from the universities,' that seems to me very much more schematic than real. Any attempt at precise articulation of the difference be-tween what a university is for and what a polytechnic is for doesn't stand up. There's a considerable overlap and there is a

*See p. 61, n. 21.   †See pp. 25.

‡The system of higher education that divides between independent uni-versities conferring their own degrees and receiving funds from the D E S on the recommendation of the University Grants Committee, and the local-authority-maintained further education polytechnics, further education colleges and colleges of education. (There are also voluntary colleges of education which receive grants directly from the DES.) See pp. 193–5 for Crosland's discussion of the binary system.

ridiculous idea, which I fear is rather prevalent in the DES at the moment that no universities are interested in teaching. Of course much the most important single difference between the universities, on the one hand, and the polytechnics and the colleges of education, on the other, is that the 'non-autonomous' institutions have so much less money for research. Perhaps the essence of the work of a university could be summed up as 'teaching in the atmosphere of research'.

Can you summarize for us the main roles that the Department ought to be playing? What is the Department's role in the education service, as you saw it?

The most important single role is fighting for the resources necessary to make a reality of more equal educational opportunity – defined in a stronger sense today than we used to think. It isn't just a matter of providing what is required to do justice to talents we are born with – it's something rather subtler than that. It's recognizing the interaction between what we are born with and how and where we grow up and all the time using the education service, not just to do justice to talents, but to help expand the supply of national talent, and, as I put it earlier on, to get away from the situation in which boys and girls are allowed to write themselves off below their true potential of ability. The Ministry of Education wants to be *the* sponsoring Department for as many young people as possible going up the educational ladder as far as their potential abilities can carry them. This has been a fight all along. There is a point that Lord James has made before now (he wouldn't agree with all I've been saying) and that is that the doctrine of interaction between nature and nurture, and that education is about the combination of the two, goes back a very long way in our civilization to the Ancient Greeks. The Department has to fight for more resources for the educational priority areas and for the city centre areas. Of all forms of injustice, the single one I find myself most riled by is the suggestion that immigrants are responsible for all social problems of the city centre areas, a suggestion that is both dangerous and quite intolerably unfair. The growth of the number of those who are visible immigrants, so to speak, has simply drawn our attention to many of these problems more acutely in the city centre areas. Then there is the old question of doing justice to children's potential talents at the primary age – the thing that the Plowden Committee was concerned about – I suspect there's more to primary education even than Plowden suggested, that Basil Bernstein and his Critical Learning Periods are important as well. Then there's making a reality of secondary education for all. We certainly shan't do that until the school-leaving age is raised. And then there are the implications of this for further education and for university education.

Now you asked me what was the role of the Department. It's fighting for resources for all this that is its most important role. I don't say all these resources should be produced by the central government – this is a matter for local government, too.

The other function of the Ministry is to act as a clearing house of ideas in the field of education, to know, to be in touch with, the best that is being thought and to help teachers over curriculum and methods – I hope we shall see a continued future for the Schools Councils which I think is an important powerhouse of development.* It links, or should be allowed to link with in-service training – helping teachers over curriculum and methods and defying, or putting the opposite point of view to, those voices that say, 'Really everything's been getting a little worse during the last forty years, and therefore teachers shouldn't be allowed, or given any encouragement, to adopt new methods.'

What about inspectors, HMIs – what role do you see for them? There are five hundred of them recruited from among the best of the teaching professions. How far did they contribute towards the polices that you made as Minister? What would you see as their role now?

We've said nothing about them in this discussion up till now and I fear that rather tells its own tale. Looking back over the period we're thinking of, about fifteen years, the Inspectorate has played less of a part in policy making than I for one would have liked to see. I think this was certainly true over

*See p. 67.

the whole question of secondary reorganization. When I look back to my time at the Ministry, I associate inspectors a lot with the briefing I got from going to particular schools, as local informants about schools. Sometimes they played an active part in Ministerial discussions, for example, Cyril English, the first FE, as it were, Senior Chief Inspector.* I suspect it's been a bigger role in some local authorities – for example when the London inspectors came before the Education Select Committee, they gave rather an impressive performance, I thought.

Might this be because of the structural arrangements within the Department? The Permanent Secretary alone has the right to direct access to the Secretary of State. The SCI is of deputy secretary rank and all promotions are formally approved by the Permanent Secretary. He is not the equivalent of, for example, the Chief Medical Officer to the Ministry of Health, or the Chief of the Imperial General Staff in the Ministry of Defence.

I think this may well be so. I don't think there was a sufficiently strong tradition that when you had a major discussion the Senior Chief Inspector should normally be invited in. Equally, I'm afraid I must say in fairness, I think there may have been personal reasons over the years why this tended not to happen. But for whatever reason, he didn't play a big enough part in policy making in the Department, whoever he was. The sad thing was that occasionally one would meet an inspector, say on the train, a senior one, who would talk interestingly and extremely fairly about any of these questions. I'm really thinking about the position in Curzon Street itself.

HMIs are one source of advice to the Department and, to some extent, to the Minister. What about such bodies as the Central Advisory Councils for Education, the National Advisory Council for the Training and Supply of Teachers, and the many other national advisory councils established under statute? Did they affect the policies you put through?

*Cyril English was Senior Chief Inspector until 1967. He is now Director-General, City and Guilds Institute.

Oh, I think there's no doubt the successive reports produced by the Central Advisory Council were very important. In fact the reality worked out differently here from the law; you didn't have a continuing Advisory Council, you had a series of ad hoc groups appointed to do that work, consider one part of the service after the other. There was, first of all, the report on early leaving, which first discussed those who were writing themselves off – or being written off – by early leaving.* Then there was the *Crowther Report* which had a great effect, not only on policy about the school-leaving age but also about further education in 1961 – that White Paper directly reflected Crowther. Then there was Newsom in 1963 which was perhaps a slightly disappointing report in some ways – but, nonetheless, it did arouse the conscience of the nation. It did make people realize ... how far we were from achieving secondary education for all. Then there was Plowden which was the first of those reports backed up by proper research and some adequate costing and feasibility planning.† One thing that bothered me was the gap in the resources that had been made available to the Robbins team compared to the resources available to Newsom, so Plowden was backed up by a proper research fund. I think these have been all important reports and, of course, they've been very much studied not only in this country, but in many other countries too. Incidentally, let's remember Robbins was set up on the instance of Eccles arising out of debate in the House of Lords. One of the few rather important major social reports that originated in the debate in the House of Lords, initiated by Lord Simon of Wythenshawe. The National Advisory Council on the Training and Supply of Teachers did a vital job at a vital time, in making us think in terms of much bigger target numbers. I was personally sorry when it ceased to exist and nothing put in its place.‡ The discipline of an ad hoc group sitting for some time, is considerable; I don't regard this most recent planning

*See p. 61, n. 18.

†For the *Crowther Report* see p. 61, n. 3. The White Paper is *Teachers for Further Education: Report of an Advisory Sub-Committee*, H M S O, 1961. For the *Newsom Report* see p. 60, n. 5. For the *Plowden Report* see p. 60, n. 7.

‡See p. 173 for Crosland's view of its lapse.

document on higher education numbers nearly as satisfactory as the Robbins appendices, with all their limitations.* It isn't only the reports. If you read the evidence given to Robbins, it is fascinating reading. Much of Plowden is of the same order. The research on what makes a good school – parental attitudes and the other variables – and the whole of that second volume is important stuff.

One advantage of having the councils which made these reports was that they brought outside people to make judgements and recommendations on policy. They also brought in the great flow of new educational sociological research from *Early Leaving* onwards. Moreover, am I right in thinking that in appointing Plowden, for the first time you deliberately brought in a sociologist or professor of social administration (D. V. Donnison), a child development expert (J. M. Tanner) and the Professor of Logic at Oxford (A. J. Ayer) to deliberately make a broad inter-disciplinary mix?† Now, why didn't you do the same thing within the Department? Unlike your successors, you never brought in economists or sociologists; was this that it simply hadn't occured to you at that time?

No, it didn't occur to me at that time to bring them in. Looking back, I think I would have brought somebody in – not many people, but I think just one person in – of my own. On the composition of the Plowden Committee – this seemed to me rather like ploughing back capital. All this work in the early 1960s was pure again, and we wanted to get some of them together – Tanner, Young, Ayer, Raison, Donnison and the CASE representative – to make more capital for the future.‡

I'd received the first deputation of CASE and I'd been much impressed by them. It was the first time a parents' movement was deliberately brought into one of these committees. Professor Ayer was slightly different. It wasn't just that I thought we ought to have a philosopher, but here was a highly intelligent

*Education Planning Paper No. 2, *Student Numbers in Higher Education*, H M S O, October 1970.

†See p. 47.

‡C A S E is the Confederation for the Advancement of State Education.

man interested in education and I remember writing to him and saying we'd seen him in the role of radical critic of society for a long time and would he consider doing some constructive work.

The composition of that committee does reflect the whole change of attitude to education that has been going on for some years, and which you, in a sense, embodied – the widening of the educational constituency. Could I turn now to the relationships between the Department and the important pressure groups with which it works? For example, Sir William Alexander, Secretary to the Association for Education Committee; the Education Officer of the ILEA.* Their equivalents in the Association of Municipal Corporations, the County Councils Association, too, must have become as well acquainted with Departmental thinking and, indeed, as consulted about it as any of your senior officials. And similarly with the National Union of Teachers and the other teacher associations. Their officials are extremely experienced and they're in their posts a long while, much longer than Ministers, or for that matter Permanent Secretaries. What effect do they have on the process of policy making and decision making within the Department?

A very considerable effect. I think, looking back over my time, it was quite a limited number of officials who had a major impact. Sir William Alexander had a vast knowledge of the education system. He was constantly in the Department as a visitor. He had the advantage, with his editor Stuart Maclure, that they had a weekly paper *Education* the journal of the Association of Education Committees, which was not just a sounding board, but it was read by everybody who was 'in' in the maintained school world, and the world of the local authorities.† And I think I'd emphasize most Sir William's great knowledge of the system. He wasn't inflexible – there were occasions when he would change his mind on a subject, rather

*Throughout the whole of Boyle's association with education Sir William Houghton was Education Officer to the London County Council at the Inner London Education Authority.

†Stuart Maclure is now the editor of *The Times Educational Supplement.*

abruptly, and this was not necessarily a fault – I think he was rather like one or two politicians I can think of – I mean no disrespect when I say he had something of the quality of Dick Crossman in him, of seeing a strong case for arguing one way at one moment, and then changing later on. For example, I can remember a time when he was against middle schools, and then, later, he was inclined to think that nine to thirteen schools, or else the sixth-form college, both had merits. But one often could try things on him knowing here was some-body of enormous knowledge and experience of how the whole complicated mechanism of government and local au-thority, how this worked from the local authority side.

I think, however, the one thing one had to be careful of as Minister, after talking with Sir William, or with some other people in local government, was not to sound too much like the spokesman in Parliament for the maintained schools. The occupational danger for a Minister was to become too much the spokesman for the maintained schools and to forget that there were other aspects of education – the public schools, for instance – on which one was expected as a Minister to have some point of view. But nonetheless, it was useful having this world coming into a focus so clearly in the person of Sir William. Now and then rather absurd attempts used to be made by other association leaders to be a sort of equal with Sir William. Well, I mean, they just weren't and Ministers in this way have got to deal with realities. Even if on paper they ought to have counted relatively for more at Curzon Street and the Association of Education Committees for less, the fact remains that it simply didn't. I remember Sir William Alexander saying to me once when we were having a sharp dis-agreement about something and I said, 'I hope this won't inhibit us from having discussions on other things,' and he said to me, 'Sir Edward, this is my life,' really in rather an impressive way. 'The idea that I wouldn't be willing to discuss with you because of our present disagreement any other sub-ject connected with public education is like asking that I should be a different person.' He once said to me that educa-tion could be rather a strong virus, but once you got it, you didn't easily get rid of it. He said, 'I've no doubt Sir Edward caught it.' There were other people too who carried weight. Sir Ronald Gould, obviously, as the General Secretary of the NUT, Houghton and Briault of London.* London, to a Minister of Education, is like a self portrait – it's always there when you want it. It's on top of you.

Of one or two other directors of education I would single out Sir Alec Clegg, Chief Education Officer of the West Riding, who carried weight simply by sheer force of being who he was, the person he was, and who made himself the spokesman of the Newsom child and the spokesman of the less fortunate in our society.† He didn't just go on about the less fortunate, he became the accepted conscience of Curzon Street in this way.

We used to say, when something was proposed, 'What would Alec Clegg think about this.' You get into that kind of position – this is my point – where it's like being, if you like, a liberal in the anti-racialist movement. It isn't on paper, you don't play for that kind of position; you either have it or you don't have it. There were a few people, who didn't always agree with one another, or with the Ministry, like Alexander, Sir Ronald Gould, Alec Clegg, who had a position which nobody gave them; they simply had it, commanded it.

Could we turn now to relations with civil servants? There is the popular assumption about bureaucratic obstructionism. How did *you* conceive their role? What attitudes did they take towards policy initiatives that you might want to have taken?

Perhaps I could go back to the Treasury for a moment here. I never recall this happening at the Department of Education, I really cannot remember an occasion when I felt I met Departmental obstructionism. I ran into difficulties from the point of view of money, not having the money to do all that one would have liked, but I can't really recall a sort of bureaucratic obstructionism. I can remember one occasion at the Treasury when both Mr Macmillan (who was then Chancellor of the Exchequer) and I felt that we ought seriously to con-

*For Houghton see p. 134. Eric Briault is Deputy Education Officer of the I L E A.

†Sir Alec Clegg was a member of the Crowther and Newsom Committees.

sider a certain policy − it was a change in taxation − and it was the emotional feelings of one senior person − not the head of the Treasury or the Chief Economic Adviser − who pushed us off it, even though practically everybody else round the table would have liked it. And I think just occasionally at the Treasury you did feel that Ministers were told 'You can't have such and such', when what they were really being told was 'I don't want you to have such and such and if I fight hard for my point of view, you won't get it'.

What Can a Secretary of State Achieve?

In fact Ministers, if they really want something, will always get it, including changes in legislation?

Oh, yes, but in practice it isn't quite so simple as that. When Ministers are bracing themselves to cross a difficult hurdle − difficult politically as well as in terms of administration − and they meet official discouragement, then it becomes far more probable that the hurdle will be avoided.

Did you feel that you had real control over this vast range of policies that the Department covers?

No, I can't say I felt I had control over it. Partly because while there were some parts of education which I did feel I came to understand reasonably well, there were other parts, particularly on the technical education side, the management studies side, for example, that I felt I never grasped in the same way. Whereas the Eccles revolution in technical education made a great difference to education for more efficient production, I think that management education was and is still in its infancy.

Can you take a number of the most important policies in education and say what was *your* role in the six or seven issues that really mattered? Was it you or was it civil servants who created the policies? Who took the initiative in making them?

Two or three occur to me straight away. The first was getting the expansion of teacher training in the early part of 1963. I personally attribute that decision to the quality of Mr Pile's briefing, the present Permanent Secretary, more than to anybody else.* Without his briefing, I don't think it would have happened. I think the decision about the raising of the school-leaving age in 1964, setting a definite date for that which, alas, afterwards got postponed – I think that was more directly due to me in the sense that I had no doubt it was the right decision to take; it was generally though not quite unanimously supported in the office, and by progressive thought outside; some economists, as you know, had very considerable doubts – and still have. But I think that was one where it was up to me, first of all, to see that the case was set out as persuasively as possible. The chief weakness of the *Newsom Report* was although it assumed the school-leaving age of sixteen it never set out arguments for it. The *Crowther Report* did. But the *Newsom Report* was the one in everybody's mind at that time. It came up and gave the right impetus just at that moment. It was my job both to take the decisions in the office and to see the case got set out well. When something is really important to you, in a Cabinet decision, you've got, not actually to draft the paper yourself, but you've got to see it's done how you want it. You've got to have meeting after meeting until you get the paper with which you're satisfied. It's no good just leaving it to other people – I always like the story of a former Cabinet Minister who, after reading rather a brilliant paper of Macmillan's, said, 'Why can't *my* Cabinet papers look like that?' Your cabinet papers *won't* look like that unless you've worked on them yourself and got other people to work on them. And therefore, getting the paper written and then fighting it through Cabinet, this one was definitely up to me.

This is, in fact, an example of where the civil service must run out of gas and where only the Minister can act?

I remember a thing which Herbert Andrew – my then Permanent Secretary – said to me, 'The difficulty you'll have with this one is that nobody's going to argue against you on

*Now Sir William Pile, Permanent Under-Secretary of the DES; at that time he was Under-Secretary in charge of teacher supply.

your grounds but they'll be arguing against you on quite different ground from those you've considered in your paper.' You've got to anticipate the sort of arguments that will be used. For instance, one tiresome one which kept on coming up from one Cabinet colleague was that it was no good giving children anything to do on paper, you only wanted to give them things to do with their hands. But, Herbert Andrew very helpfully did me a paper about what Newsom called 'The Robinsons', the least able, those who really were going to be troublesome.* There was one argument it used: at that time it looked as though, short of raising the school-leaving age, you weren't going to get as many as 50 per cent staying on voluntarily to sixteen, at that time over the country as a whole. We already had the CSE examination so that we were fully geared to cope with 60 per cent of those who would be staying on when the age was raised. As for the remainder, well, we had the beginnings of a curriculum for them. The *Newsom Report*, whatever its other limitations, had some useful stuff about the curriculum for the really less able. The evidence in *Newsom* suggested that, if we were God, we would probably have raised the age for about 93 per cent, something like that; 'The Robinsons' were not more than about 7 per cent. Taking all these figures together, it seemed to me clear that the waste of human potential involved in not raising the age was clearly greater than the administrative problems that would be raised by doing it. And, of course, another piece of good luck I had was the concern felt about the North East at that moment; one could so convincingly portray that even if this move wasn't absolutely necessary for Kent, or even for London, it was simply vital for Northumberland and Durham. It happened that the decision coincided with Lord Hailsham and his cloth-cap visits up to the North-East.†

*The Robinsons were three mythical children who appear in ch. 22 of the *Newsom Report* (see p. 60, n. 5). They came from 'the bottom quarter of ability'.

†Harold Macmillan appointed Lord Hailsham to coordinate the government's efforts in stimulating the economic and social development of the North-East.

These are examples of policies that you put through and they show the civil servant, in fact, presenting arguments to the point where a judgement has to be made. Every other Minister had a scheme that could have been put in instead of raising the school leaving age. Only Ministers can make the allocation as between those priorities at that point.

As a matter of fact, if I remember rightly, at Cabinet, it was one of those curious mornings when we had three things before us – I think decimalization was another – and it was one of those mornings when you decide at the beginning of the day you can't afford any of them and by one o'clock you've decided you're going to afford all of them.

January Sales. From what you have said there are certainly distinctions between civil service and Ministerial roles. The process seems to emerge as one of rational discourse between permanent experts and yourself, taking decisions as a result of a rational process. Is that the flavour of the system as you re-call it?

Yes indeed. I think that's just as I would describe it. I don't recall a single occasion at Curzon Street when I had to say 'This is a Ministerial decision.' I once recall this happening on a relatively small matter at the Treasury. I imagine when the public think about this situation they're thinking of a sort of big policy issue. It's actually, I think, much more likely to happen on a relatively small matter. On one small matter when I was Financial Secretary I happened to take just the opposite view to my predecessor, Jack Simon – it was quite a small thing – but he was in disagreement with the Ministry of Works on a point – I thought Hugh Molson of the Ministry of Works was right.* And just on that occasion I said, 'No, I'm sorry – this is the new Ministerial decision,' and there was just a day or two of slight fuss about it ... but it didn't last. But that's the only time I can remember this happening in fifteen years.

*Lord Simon was Financial Secretary, 1958–9 and President of the Admiralty, Divorce and Probate Division of High Court until March 1971. Hugh Molson, now Lord Molson, was Minister of Works, 1957–9.

One could construe this as civil servants so able to run their Ministers that no need ever arises for Ministers to exert themselves in this way?

Indeed, and of course, this can happen. Officials are, obviously, more skilled, or less skilled, at handling Ministers. But officials like Ministers to know their own minds, and I just don't recognize in Lord Snow's novels Ministerial life as I've known it. The patchiness of Lord Snow's experience I always think is perfectly shown in that curious moment in *Corridors of Power,* where you have a major decision of a Cabinet committee taken on government expenditure with no Treasury representation present, which seems to me very implausible. But of course some officials are clever at handling Ministers, just as some Ministers are clever at getting the best out of civil servants; but I don't, however, believe most officials these days want to feel they're all the time persuading Ministers against their will. I think they may, at times, feel that Ministers don't realize the logic of where their own policies are leading, and you've just simply got to make them realize what this does imply for policy. Ministers, just like some politicians, are quite capable of saying 'I want X', and you say 'Oh, but X means Y', and he'll say 'Oh, but I don't want Y' – that could happen with Ministers just as it can with backbenchers.

You're not really very hot on conflict theory? All of this dialogue brings out that you don't really see much conflict between bureaucracy and the electoral process as represented by Ministers?

I don't think a conflict-free society is possible. I quite understand a lot of people might think I was very 'repressively tolerant'. I haven't been involved politically in all those many Departments where this subject, what you're talking about, is particularly relevant. If we're going to talk about conflict, it was more between me and a certain section of my party, though, as I've said, nothing like all of it. I don't think though, as I played the hand, there was much conflict between myself as a politician, with pressures behind me, and officials. My advisers and I were not engaged in a joint racket against humanity, if I can put it that way. There were frequently times when we should have fought harder for resources, and there were many occasions when I gave vent to, if you like, generalized humanistic sentiments, when I didn't fight quite as hard as I should have done to clothe them in realities of money and bricks and mortar and all that. I'm quite prepared to agree with anyone who says that I didn't live up to my principles as well as I should, just as some advisers were perhaps a bit cynical about what could be done. And we all probably thought a bit too much in terms of individual values rather than collective values, I mean very few of us Ministers had any first-hand knowledge of the trade unions. All those things may be true, but the idea that we were engaged in a sort of conspiracy against humanity, or that a different lot of Ministers, differently chosen, would have done all that much better in this respect, I find awfully difficult to believe. I hope it's not complacent to say this, at a time when it is suggested that the whole 'system' is a racket. I have quite a lot of sympathy with the youth of this country whose more militant members feel they are showing up the hypocrisy of society – I sympathize with anyone who finds it distasteful. For instance, I think there is an element of hypocrisy in the way a lot of people talk about South Africa today. A great many people who say they're against apartheid do, in their inmost being, feel that a successful capitalist country can't be really all that wrong, and with just a bit of encouragement it could change rather easily. There may well have been some hypocrisy in the way we carried on in the Ministry. But I definitely don't believe we were all engaged in an exercise of semi-conscious hypocrisy.

So the networks between you and civil servants didn't seem to be a sort of Establishment – if not conspiring, then at least sharing assumptions so comfortably and glibly that it was a silent, or unconscious, conspiracy.

That's right. We were, at times, I think, all of us prepared to be anti-Establishment, prepared a bit to be rebels, if you like. There always had to be an element of the 'anti-government' about the Ministry of Education – fighting for resources at times other people found inconvenient. And I think we were prepared to do that at the cost of quite a bit of time and quite a bit of intellectual and moral discomfort. This was certainly true of Eccles, who was often extremely courageous. It was true of officials, like Weaver, arguing with the Treasury in three four-hour meetings before getting those extra eight thousand training college places after Crowther. I think Tyrrell Burgess's tribute to the Department of Education, that we did try to view this subject from the outside inwards, and not from the inside outwards – I think that was broadly true.*

*Tyrrell Burgess, *New Society*, 12 September 1963.

Anthony Crosland

**Interviewed on 7 September and 6 October 1970
at his London home**

Anthony Crosland was Minister of State for Economic Affairs
from October 1964 (a post combined with the office of
Economic Secretary to the Treasury) and was Secretary of
State for Education and Science between January 1965 and
August 1967, when he became President of the Board
of Trade.

Introduction

Labour assumed office in October 1964 in the midst of a
balance of payments crisis which dogged economic policy
making throughout its period in office. Balance of payments
deficits ran from £278 million in 1965, to £67 million
in 1966 to £461 million in 1967. Every new set of poor
trade statistics sparked off pressure on sterling. Income
restraint was a key policy. Innovations such as the setting
up of the Industrial Reorganization Corporation in
1966 were aimed at future growth and the concept of the
National Plan was 'purposeful' development, but the
six-and-a-half week seamen's strike shortly after the 1966
Budget brought about another wave of pressure on the
pound. The tide had turned against sterling, and finally, in
November 1967, the pound was devalued. In Samuel
Brittan's view it was a 'well planned and well carried out
operation' but in another overall analysis Brian Lapping
has maintained that 'the final judgement on the economic
policies of Labour must be unfavourable. During a period
when world trade was expanding fast, Britain under Labour
took less than her fair share of the growth in trade'.*

Whatever assessment should be made of Labour's
performance, the period 1965–7 was crisis ridden and
economically austere. Stringent deflation, despite the

*For Samuel Brittan see p. 65. Brian Lapping's quotation is from *The
Labour Government: 1964–1970*, Penguin, 1970.

'false dawns' during this period, contrasted strongly with the optimistic and buoyant expansionism of 1962–4.

It was in this economic climate, in which technical mistakes produced disproportionately disastrous consequences, and in which the government tried to reconcile conflicting objectives of realignment of the economy towards fundamental growth, redistribution to the needy, and retention of international confidence, that Anthony Crosland had to pursue radical, and particularly expensive, policies.

The main events of Crosland's period of office at the Department were:

1965   Issued *Circular 10/65* which called attention to the government's declared objective to end selection at 11-plus and to eliminate separation in secondary education. It 'requested' local education authorities 'to submit plans for their areas on these lines within a year'.

Announced programmes of long-term research by National Foundation for Educational Research into methods of organizing comprehensive schools and an assessment of their achievements by the University of Manchester.

Circular 7/65 reaffirmed view 'that immigrant children have a legal right to education according to age, ability and aptitude'.

Established first Public Schools Commission, under Sir John Newsom's chairmanship 'to advise on the best way of integrating the public schools with the state system of education'.

Made speech to NUT Annual Conference announcing fourteen points by which teacher recruitment and deployment could be improved. Wrote to the colleges calling for the adoption of measures to make more productive use of facilities so as to step up their output of trained teachers by 20 per cent.

Wrote 'personal' letter to 10,000 potential 'returners',

Woolwich speech to Association of Teachers in
Technical Institutions accepted the binary concept of
higher education.

1966   White Paper announcing intention to designate thirty
Polytechnics.

1967   Plowden and Gittins Committees reported.

Building programme of £16 million announced
for educational priority areas.

Creation of National Council for Educational
Technology.

Creation of Social Science Research Council.

Creation of the Planning Branch of the Department
of Education and Science.

Circular on overseas students' fees.

Announced that university accounts would be open
to scrutiny by Comptroller and Auditor-General.

Anthony Crosland

The Attraction of Politics

You were an Oxford don before you went into politics. You stayed in politics while the going was rough as well as good. You could have chosen between many careers. What is the lure of politics to someone such as yourself?

I wanted to go into politics, and specifically Labour politics, ever since I was about seventeen. Without going into any psychological explanation – if there is one I don't know what it is! – I have always held very strong views about public affairs and have wanted a chance to influence them. I wanted to be involved in the actual process of taking decisions and making policies. This seemed to me, and still seems to me, more satisfactory than writing books about them from an Oxford chair.

Did you ever consider any alternatives? You were able to affect decision making and policy making as a Minister. But there are other ways of doing this too. Beveridge, Titmuss, Tawney or Kaldor are examples of those who found them. Did you balance those chances, or was it always politics?

Politics were always the first choice, though their lead over the second choice was sometimes a bit narrow. The second choice for me was in fact writing. There was a time when I think I probably did waver. This was after I had written *The Future of Socialism*, had worked on the Co-op report and had written some of *The Conservative Enemy*.* I had been out of the House for a time, and I wasn't absolutely certain that I wanted to come back in 1959. There was a previous period of slight wavering when I was a don from 1947 to 1950. I suppose one's priorities are bound to be different at different stages of

*For *The Future of Socialism* see p. 61, n 10. The 'Co-op report' refers to the Co-operative Independent Commission, *Report*, Co-operative Union Ltd, 1958. For *The Conservative Enemy* see p. 51.

one's development. But for most of the time I have wanted to be in politics, and I certainly don't want to leave them now.

Politicians want to have an influence on affairs of state – perhaps to change the world. But civil servants, too, have a major influence on policies. Why not aim to be a top civil servant – a Permanent Secretary rather than a Cabinet Minister, an Assistant Secretary rather than an MP? The arithmetical chance of getting there is better anyway, and you are likely to have a longer period of influence.

I'm not sure how the arithmetical chances compare, but the answer, I would think, is twofold. It's partly a matter of temperament. Some people prefer the more orderly and administrative life and work of the civil servant. Others are temperamentally drawn to the more chaotic but exciting public life of a Minister or politician. That's part of it. The other reason is that politicians convince themselves that as Ministers they will be carrying out their own policies, whereas as civil servants they would merely be carrying out someone else's policies. Put like that it's of course a grossly over-simplified view, but there's a reality behind it.

The choice is between trying to change policies rather than working out the consequences?

Well, let me take an example. If, as an official, you believe in comprehensive reorganization, you can't by yourself introduce it as a national policy. That can only be done by a Minister backed by his party. Certainly the official will have great influence on the way the policy is carried out, on what happens in Plymouth or Stockport or somewhere. But the crucial decision can be taken only by a Minister.

Is this quite true? What about Morant or, more recently, Morrell or Nenk.* Or, say, the Deputy Secretaries you worked

*Sir Robert Morant was Permanent Secretary to the Board of Education, 1903–11. He was a tutor to princes in Siam before joining the Board of Education. He was thought to be the principal author with Arthur Balfour of the Education Act, 1902. He was Chairman of the Insurance Commission which implemented the 1911 Insurance Act.

with so well? Are they not innovators who have actually changed or originated major policies? Surely they have helped mould policies over a long period of years?

There will always be the occasional administrator who originates and promotes important policies. But if the policies are at all controversial, he can't get very far unless a Minister backs him. Even the most passive Minister fulfils the role of occasionally saying, 'No – that's just not on politically.' What it comes to is this. An active Minister will himself initiate changes in policy; while even a passive Minister exercises a final right of veto. In either case the Ministerial role is crucial – which of course isn't to devalue the equally crucial but quite different role of the administrator.

You say that the difference between politicians and civil servants is partly a matter of temperament. Could you tell me more about these differences?

I think there are probably two. The politician has got to have, or try to acquire, an extremely thick skin. Unlike the civil servant, he is constantly going to be attacked in Parliament, criticized in the press, heckled at public meetings, badgered by endless and often hostile deputations. If he's lucky, of course, he may also be praised occasionally – that's one of the compensations! But he has to have a particular sort of toughness, robustness and resilience.

The second difference is that the politician's life is exceedingly insecure. He will spend some time finding a seat in the first place, nursing it, and getting elected. Then he's liable to lose his seat, as I did in 1955, and has got to find another one and get elected again. If he becomes a Minister he will suddenly lose his job because his party is chucked out of office at a General Election, as I did by the decision of the electorate on 18 June 1970. If I look back on my life, insecurity has been a very marked characteristic. This is not true of the civil servant – he may fail to become a Permanent Secretary but he is never going to lose his job. Perhaps unfortunately.

What effect does the insecurity have upon the thinking of the politician? It obviously affects his judgement on priorities? The fact that he is working within a pattern of insecurity might, for example, mean a difference in the pace with which the civil servant moves towards objectives and the politician towards them. Or the scale of the objectives. Because you have such a short time, relatively speaking, when you are in power, does it mean that you have to have an urgency behind what you want to do with the system generally?

I think it's true that the politician is always in more of a hurry because he knows that his time as a Minister may be limited. But this is part of his function in any case, particularly if he belongs to a reforming party. He *should* be constantly pushing and prodding and asking why things haven't been done. That's one of the things he's there for.

Becoming a Cabinet Minister

When you became Secretary of State it was your first Cabinet job. Gordon Walker had been defeated in the Leyton by-election on a Thursday night. By Friday you had ceased to be Minister of State at the Department of Economic Affairs. Overnight you stepped into control of a great Department of State. Did you have any clear view of the educational policies you wanted to put into effect?

In the sense of being an expert educationalist with detailed knowledge, no. In terms of certain broad principles and policy objectives, yes. I had written chapters on educational policy both in *The Future of Socialism* and *The Conservative Enemy.** I had definite views, for example, on comprehensive reorganization, on the public schools, on the expansion of higher education, and on the priority to be given to education as a whole; and I knew that teacher supply was the most urgent and immediate task. But in no sense had I expert views on detailed policies, for example on how best to develop further education, or how in detail to increase teacher supply, or what should be done about the organization of science. I certainly knew far less than Michael Stewart, who had been a

*See chs. 10 and 11, respectively.

teacher and also front-bench opposition spokesman on education, or Ted Short, who was a former headmaster.

You were the person with authority to express a clear view about what social and other changes ought to be effected through the educational system. No one else within the Department – apart from the junior Ministers – had, as it were, licence to articulate and promote these principles? Was it this that differentiated you from the civil servants?

Certainly it's the first task of an incoming Minister to lay down clearly what his party's policy is; and that policy will be based on certain principles and values. It's then the task of the civil service to scrutinize this policy in terms of feasibility. The civil servants will, incidentally, already have a very good idea of what your party's policies are. They will have read the party manifesto. If the incoming Minister has written something himself they would have the sense to read it over the weekend after he had come into office! If the government has just changed they will already have used the election period to prepare briefs based on your party's known policies. So you don't have to assemble them all in a room and give them a solemn lecture. You simply have to make it clear as decisions come up that these are the basic policies and you propose to stick to them.

Were these policies developed by the Labour Party in opposition, or were they personal to you?

Well, they were personal to me in the sense that I had thought and written a good deal about basic educational objectives. But they were also in line with official Labour Party thinking. There was no conflict here.

Were you able to predict the limitations on a Cabinet Minister's ability to effect his own policies?

I'm not sure how accurately I predicted them beforehand. But I had naturally thought a great deal about politics for a long time and had observed them at least from a backbencher's seat. I had also been close to a number of people

who had been Ministers in the post-War Labour government –
Dalton in one generation, Gaitskell in another. And I knew
quite a lot of civil servants who had been contemporaries at
university. So I probably had a rough commonsense perception of how the thing worked, but of course no detailed knowledge based on personal experience.

Hugh Dalton quotes Arthur Henderson as saying, 'The first
forty-eight hours decide whether a Minister is going to run
his office, or whether his office is going to run him.' And Dalton himself adds that 'a Minister should show his officials at the
start that he has a mind of his own'.* Do you share this view?

I think the view is sometimes interpreted rather theatrically
and over-dramatically. Arthur Henderson's quotation has become very familiar to politicians, and I think that a lot of incoming Ministers feel they must make some immediate dramatic
gesture to impress the Department with their strong personality –
like saying all the furniture must be changed, or demanding a different lavatory from the one they've got, or asking that the whole of
their private office should be reshuffled. I don't think this sort of
thing much impresses civil servants; they see through it, and I
imagine give a smile of tolerant amusement. What is important is
that at an early stage officials should see that you're not willing to
accept submissions automatically and without any question, but
that you propose to criticize, to reject when you think necessary,
and to take initiatives of your own. In other words they must
see that you have a mind of your own and are determined to
take the final decision yourself. Whether they'll see this in the
first forty-eight hours or not I really don't know, but they
will certainly form a view very quickly. And of course, to be
realistic, there's another point. If you've been a Minister before, officials of your new department will know on the Whitehall grapevine in considerable detail what you are like, so
that this chest-beating necessity in any case applies only to the
first Ministerial job which someone gets.

When you are appointed Secretary of State, to the outside

*See Boyle's reply to this question, p. 79.

world you seem to be the person making all the major decisions. But you must feel suddenly plunged into a vast area – much of which is bound to be foreign to you.

That's absolutely true. If you're conscientious as a Minister and want to get things right, your first few days in a Department are likely to be fairly hellish – so much to do, so much to learn, so little time to learn it in before you have to start making detailed decisions. My wife tells me I was always acutely depressed during my first few days in a new Department. I reckon it takes you six months to get your head properly above water, a year to get the general drift of most of the field, and two years really to master the whole of a Department.

The pressure is on to make instant decisions? This must be terrifying.

It is rather alarming. What you try to do is concentrate on those subjects which need quick decisions and postpone the rest. My wife keeps a very erratic diary. After I'd been at Curzon Street four weeks she noted:

Tony came home tonight with red box No. 3. 'If I had more Ministers and more time it would be fun, but it's not now.' Evidently a long day of X talking interminably in Cabinet and fresh papers piling up as fast as earlier ones are dealt with. Advent of Jennie Lee clearly going to be an additional complication. 'To tell you the truth, I'm not frightfully interested in the arts at this moment in time.' I reminded him that last week he told me after a dinner with Vice-Chancellors all asking for more money: 'To tell you the truth, I'm not frightfully interested in the universities at this moment.' And the week before when Vaizey etc. etc. had all accosted him on the subject of the public schools: 'If the truth be known, I'm not frightfully interested in the public schools at this moment.' He denies he ever said it, but he did – probably because 1. he has an extravagant mode of speech, 2. his powers of concentration are extreme (and can be exclusive), 3. in fact he does think only teacher supply and the comprehensive issue deserve priority at this moment.

I don't know how accurate my wife is as a female Pepys, but there's a basic truth in that story. You can't possibly take everything on board at once, so you try to tackle subjects one at a time. It may be annoying for officials, but you have to say,

'I am sorry, this will have to wait.' The situation was worse at the Board of Trade than at Education because individual decisions came up much more frequently there. I remember Ted Redhead saying that the pace was much more leisurely at Education.* It doesn't mean that people work less hard, but you don't have nearly so many decisions that have to be made in forty-eight hours as you do at the Board of Trade.

On Being a Minister

We might come to some of the large issues that could not wait later on. But how did you spend your day or week as Secretary of State? What really took the time and effort?

This is hard to answer – days varied so much, for example according to whether the House was sitting or not. First, inside Curzon Street, a constant flow of papers, office meetings, deputations and – a terribly time-consuming thing – writing and preparing speeches for Parliament, the National Union of Teachers, the Association of Education Committees and all sorts of other conferences. Secondly, in Whitehall, meetings of Cabinet and Cabinet Committees. Thirdly, in Westminster, answering Parliamentary Questions, taking debates, meeting groups of MPs. Fourthly, a lot of evening engagements with various educational bodies. Then at weekends, apart from looking after my own constituency, which takes quite a lot of time, visits to schools, universities, colleges, local authorities. And lastly, perhaps more than most Ministers, I used to try to find time to think.

It must be rare for a Minister to be able to apply time and willpower to thinking about policies?

It's certainly extremely difficult, because Ministerial life is one constant and endless rush. I think it's probably a matter of temperament. If you've got, as I had, an academic background, or have tried serious writing, you tend to believe that problems yield to thought. I was also helped, as I think you know,

*Edward Redhead served as a Minister of State at the Board of Trade, June 1964 – October 1965, and at the DES, October 1965 – January 1967.

by having groups of private advisers around here to discuss basic issues – this forced me to think a great deal. But I dare say sustained thinking is a minority occupation amongst Ministers, though I've always found it very helpful!

How far is it possible for the Secretary of State to delegate work to junior Ministers or to other people who are near him in the office? Have junior Ministers got a real job of work to do?

All Ministers delegate a lot of detailed work to their junior Ministers – taking Adjournment Debates in the House, going to committees, seeing local as opposed to national deputations, dealing with much of the correspondence from MPs. How far you go beyond that and delegate *decisions* depends partly of course on the Minister's own desire to delegate, but mainly on the calibre of the junior Ministers you have. One simply can't generalize. I've had junior Ministers to whom I would delegate a great deal, others to whom I wouldn't delegate anything but routine trivia. But of course all *major* policy decisions have in the end to be taken by the Minister himself.

What about your principal Private Secretary? He is made available to you by the Department. He is a civil servant. His career depends on the judgements made on him by other civil servants. Is he really a part of the political system so that he is loyal primarily to the Minister or is he loyal to the Department? Isn't this really a good test of how far Ministers' and civil servants' values might conflict?

The Minister's Private Secretary is in a unique position because of his closeness to the Minister. The rest of the Department feels itself part of an ongoing machine which will survive numerous transient Ministers. But the Private Secretary is so involved in the Minister's entire life, including his political life, that he often develops a special personal loyalty – even though he'll transfer it very quickly to the Minister's successor! – separate from his loyalty to the Department. He does in fact suffer a conflict of loyalties – and the Minister needs to know how the conflict is coming out! Is he repeating your indiscreet remarks to the Permanent Secretary, or the Permanent Secretary's indiscreet remarks to you, or neither, or both? This may sound funny, but there's an important point here. An able Private Secretary who will talk about the Department with intelligent indiscretion (if I can use the phrase) is invaluable to a Minister. This is one of the quickest means whereby a Minister can learn about the strengths and weaknesses of his Department.

Can we go back to the Minister's control over policy making? You've already said it takes about two years to get full control. But policy making can be a longer haul than that. Does any Minister have long enough at Education not only to master the essentials but also to get on to the tedious job of working out long-term objectives – or seeing that they are worked out?

In your two years you can certainly lay down long-term objectives in the central fields – for example, secondary reorganization, the pattern of higher education, teacher supply, the organization of science – though of course you will seldom see them finally achieved. What you will not be able to do is to get round to every chunk of Departmental policy and approve or alter it as the case may be. There will be chunks of the Department and of Departmental policy which you have not really had time to look at at all.

It was worse at the Board of Trade. I remember Herbert Andrew quoting Peter Thorneycroft* as saying that after nearly six years at the Board of Trade he had just about managed to get round to every aspect of the Board's work. But the Board of Trade was one of the worst Departments in Whitehall from this point of view – it was a huge sprawling great conglomerate. After two years in Education you are just about in a position to have a view of the whole field and to say that in the next six months I will look at A and B and C, and in the following six months something else.

*Peter Thorneycroft (now Lord Thorneycroft) was President of the Board of Trade, October 1951–January 1957. (Lord Runciman was President for longer, November 1931–May 1937.)

If two years is the minimum, what is the maximum period?

This is hard to say. My longest period in any one job was two and a half years at Education, and I would certainly have liked more time there. So I've never had the maximum. You would have to ask Denis Healey, who had five and half years at Defence, which was perhaps too long. Maybe something over three years is the optimum. You see, there are two conflicting arguments. On the one hand there is only a limited number of Ministers – or officials – who have drive, initiative and a sense of creative impulse, and it's right that they should move periodically from one field to another. On the other hand a Minister must stay in a Department long enough not only to master it properly but also, having mastered it, to have time to devote to major policy decisions outside his own field. This happened far too little under the Labour government, and it was largely due to the fact that people were continually being switched around and so constantly having to master new Departments. I had four separate jobs in five and a half years, which was far too many.

It is probably rather unusual for a Minister to have a job for more than three years, isn't it?

Well, it is these days. It used not to be. This is quite a new thing, this constant reshuffling of Ministers. Of course there will always be compelling reasons why a Prime Minister must make periodic changes. But the changes are much more frequent now than they used to be. In Baldwin's 1924–9 government sixteen out of the twenty-one Cabinet Ministers held the same office throughout the Parliament; fifteen out of twenty did so in the 1931–5 government.

The Constraints on the Minister's Power: His Freedom of Action
What major limitations did you experience as Secretary of State for Education?

Well, there are the obvious political constraints which apply to any Minister. But if we're talking specifically about Education, I would say first the legacy of history – the material legacy of thousands of buildings and institutions of particular types and sizes; this greatly limits your freedom to make rapid changes in policy. Secondly, the high degree of autonomy of much of the educational world – the fact that power and decision making are not centralized in Whitehall but are dispersed amongst local authorities, universities, Research Councils and so on. Thirdly, the existence of strong pressure groups of all kinds, of which the local authority and teachers' associations are of course the most important and powerful. Lastly, and perpetually, not enough money – though Education did extremely well for money under both Edward Boyle and myself.

Let's take the general political constraints first. How far were you a free agent as Secretary of State? What limitations from within the government were placed on your authority by the Prime Minister, or the whole Cabinet, or the Treasury?

As far as the Prime Minister was concerned, virtually none. Harold Wilson was an excellent delegator. I think he generally approved of what I was doing and didn't feel the need to interfere. As far as the Cabinet is concerned, again, very little. I only recollect taking two matters to Cabinet – *Circular 10/65* and the Public Schools Commission – and then the discussion was very brief.* Of course Education would come up, like all the spending Departments, at the time of the annual public expenditure exercise and then there'd be argument about possible economies. But generally very few things went either to Cabinet or Cabinet Committees.

Now why? Well, for one thing, Education is a lucky Department in the sense that while of course it has interconnections everywhere, yet in some way it stands rather separate and on its own. This is certainly true as compared with the Board of Trade where practically every decision had to be argued with the Treasury or with DEA.† The other thing is that if you're carrying out agreed Party policy, and seem to be doing it reasonably successfully and without frightful rows breaking

*For *Circular 10/65* see p. 62, n. 31. For the Public Schools Commission see p. 51–2.
†The Department of Economic Affairs, where Crosland was a Minister of State, October 1964–January 1965.

out, your colleagues won't particularly want to interfere. They are all exceedingly busy men in their own jobs, and I think they were prepared to trust my judgement.

Who decides whether an issue gets to Cabinet or not?

The Prime Minister will occasionally direct that an issue should be brought to Cabinet, usually if he thinks it's going wrong. Again, if an issue involves the agreement of another Department, for example the Treasury, and this is not forthcoming, then it will automatically go to Cabinet or Cabinet Committee.

But if it's an issue which you have the right and the power to decide yourself as Minister, then it's your judgement alone as to whether you take it to your colleagues – though of course if you've got any sense you'll consult your Permanent Secretary. On the one hand you will prefer not to have to argue the matter in front of a lot of uninformed colleagues who won't have properly mastered the issue. But if it's a highly controversial and political issue, you will think it right to give your colleagues a chance to express their views. So it's always a nice matter of judgement whether you take something to Cabinet. And of course it's also a matter of temperament. Some Ministers take as little as possible to Cabinet. Others lack confidence in their political judgement and constantly want support. On the whole much too much goes to Cabinet.

There isn't much correlation between how important an issue is and how much time is spent on it in Cabinet. This may sound odd but in practice it's inevitable. The issues that take up Cabinet time are those which are controversial within the government. They may be crucially important like economic policy or a Middle East crisis, or they may be relatively narrow like how much money should be given to ailing companies. It's not their intrinsic importance, but their political content, that puts them on the Cabinet agenda.

I know many of my colleagues thought Education of the greatest importance – for one thing, the Labour government had a lot of ex-teachers in it. But they thought it was going quite well, and I was carrying out party policy. So I think they said, 'This is one sector of this damned government that is not doing too badly, really, so we don't want to have endless discussions about it in Cabinet.' Very sensible too.

So this does not mean that the Cabinet are concerned more with short-term crises in the economy or foreign affairs rather than with the duller decisions which affect long-term futures?

No. Of course short-term crises will take up a lot of time. But Cabinet certainly discusses long-term issues also. Regional policies, public investment programmes, the reorganization of local government, the third London Airport – yes, Cabinet is constantly discussing things which will profoundly affect the country ten or twenty years ahead. I don't mean that the system works ideally – far from it. The Cabinet is too large; much too much detail comes up to it; and there is no proper machinery for continuously discussing long-term economic strategy in particular. Some form of Inner Cabinet is in my view essential.

If it is up to the Minister to decide when to submit collective decision, the Secretary of State must have great individual power. He can almost go it alone.

I think that's particularly true in a Department like Education as long as you are operating broadly within the framework of party policy and things are thought to be going reasonably well. But it was very different in the Board of Trade where almost every issue that came up involved other Departments – the Treasury, DEA, Housing and Local Government, Scotland, Wales.* So you can't generalize on this. I think Education is a particularly independent Department in Whitehall. David Eccles is related to have said, after being six years in Education, that during the whole of this time there was only one educational subject that was ever discussed in Cabinet and that was the Oxford Ring Road.

This raises the general question of how far the Cabinet and the Cabinet network are, or were, when you were in office, the

*'Housing' is now the Department of the Environment.

real centres of decision making. As Haldane put it, 'the main-spring of all the mechanism of government'* Obviously that is not so.

The Haldane quotation sounds extremely peculiar. The indi-vidual Departments must surely be the mainspring of execu-tive activity. They should put up the policies, and Cabinet should accept or reject them according to whether they are consistent with general government objectives. If a Minister is not capable of being his own mainspring and initiating his own policies he should be sacked. Not, alas, that he always is.

How does the Department relate its work to other Depart-ments and the rest of the government machine?

It's the Department's job, acting under Ministerial guidance, to identify educational objectives, and I think it is quite com-petent to do so. It's then the function of inter-Departmental machinery to make sure that the educational objectives are consistent with other objectives – with the total public ex-penditure position, with regional policy, with housing and social service policy. The only other way of operating would be to have a central unit in Number Ten or the Cabinet Office which would be responsible for setting or coordinating objec-tives.

Would you favour such a unit? Would it not be better than where this is now being done – *faute de mieux* – by the Treasury which under the guise of collating expenditure de-cisions is, in effect, creating or stultifying educational objec-tives?

Well, the Treasury is, always has been, and always will be an infuriating nuisance – but an inevitable one. Obviously they must, in the interests of macro-economic policy, take a close interest in these vast blocks of expenditure. The essential thing is to stop them interfering in the priorities *within* the total educational budget.

As to a new central coordinating unit, no, I would not

*See p. 61, n. 25.

favour it. I would certainly not want such a unit to lay down educational objectives – that's the job of the Secretary of State for Education. Nor should it decide the priorities between education and housing and defence and regional policy – that's what the Cabinet is there for. There may be a case for a central capability unit such as the present government is now setting up.* But that would have a quite different function – of subjecting certain major investment decisions, such as Concorde or the RB 211 or a third London Airport, to a rigorous cost–benefit analysis.

There is an obvious gap in the machinery, but it's a different one. We now have a reasonable degree of coordination of macro-economic policy, of industrial policy and of regional–housing–transport policies. But there is still insufficient coordination and planning of social policies which affect the poor. We need a better machinery for a total and comprehensive poverty programme.

But isn't there perhaps a reluctance in this country to discuss values and objectives? The Swedes and the French aren't frightened to talk about values, whether hypocritically or not, and to pursue them through policy. Are not civil servants coy about such discussions in a way their European or American counterparts are not?

I'm surprised at what you say. I suppose the British tend to have a rather empirical cast of mind. But I never noticed any reluctance to discuss values and objectives in Curzon Street. I constantly discussed them publicly in speeches, with much help from many officials.

But did senior officials give much time to discussion of such issues as: what educational advances are needed over the next ten or twenty years; what choices between conflicting objectives – social demand or equality or economic growth – must be made? Was this type of discussion part of the political or administrative climate in your time as Secretary of State?

I don't follow you on this. I believe many officials are deeply concerned with the things you have in mind. On the other

*See p. 32.

hand it's not the job of officials to lay down what the particular values and objectives should be – whether we should have
a selective or egalitarian system of secondary education –
that's a job for Ministers.

But does that mean you're wholly satisfied with the way we
lay down our long-term objectives in this country?

No. As I've said, in a democracy these are largely – and rightly
– determined by the general ideology and outlook of the
party in power. Nevertheless, I think we could look at the
detailed criteria more systematically – in terms of logical con-
sistency, of international comparisons, and so on. This applies
particularly in the field of social policy.

Do MPs have any impact on educational policy making?

A decisive impact? Not normally. You would tend to dis-
count the views of Opposition MPs on major policy. As to
your own party, any sensible Minister keeps in very close contact. I continually talked to the Parliamentary Labour Party
Education Group, and kept in close touch with them. I tested
out policies on them and explained why I was doing what I
was. I took a lot of trouble in this way, which I'm sure was
right. There would be occasional differences with some MPs
– on binary, or how fast we should push the comprehensive
thing, and most of all on overseas students' fees. But generally I was pursuing policies of which most Labour MPs approved and which they didn't wish to change substantially.

I also consulted individual MPs a lot on local points. I frequently used to talk, or else get a junior Minister or Chris
Price who was my Parliamentary Private Secretary to talk, to
individual MPs about comprehensive schemes in their con-
stituencies. It was a good way of assessing local feeling and
getting a view which might be different from the Departmental advice. I wouldn't invariably take it but I always liked to
hear it.

Could we go to another aspect of this. Education is described
as 'distributing life chances' – the type of question that
Social Democrats are particularly interested in, yet it is said

that there is not much interest displayed in the subject by either party.* Can you comment on this?

But how do you judge? By the number of parliamentary questions? The number of debates? You'd have to do a statistical exercise comparing the number of columns of Hansard taken up by education as compared with other subjects – and remembering that the result would be heavily influenced by which Departments happened to have major Bills going through the House, which Education did not while I was there. Otherwise I don't know the evidence for your statement.

But in local authorities, education is regarded as a prime issue to be worked on. It seems to seep away nationally. There are not many major debates in Parliament, and what there are are not well attended.

I don't know how many full-scale debates there were whilst I was Minister – perhaps six in all. They weren't very well attended, but then few debates in the House of Commons are unless there's a great political row going on. This isn't at all a good index of the degree of interest. What I said earlier about the Cabinet is also true of Parliament. It spends most time on things that are going wrong or things that are acutely party-controversial, and education didn't fall into these categories at that time.

But there's one thing worth mentioning. With the changing social composition of the Parliamentary Labour Party – more ex-college lecturers and fewer ex-primary schoolteachers – there was a change in the *balance* of interest. The debate on overseas students' fees was infinitely more crowded and animated than any debate on primary schools. I doubt if this is wholly a good sign.

What about the Labour Party's role in policy making?

If you mean Transport House, this is not very large when

*Quotation from the Introduction to A. H. Halsey, J. Floud and C. Arnold, *Education, Economy and Society: A Reader in the Sociology of Education*, Free Press, 1961.

Labour is in government simply because a Minister has access to far greater resources in the civil service. When we were in opposition Transport House did set up the Taylor working party on higher education, of course, but when you're in power the policy-making role of the party is bound to be limited.* In opposition it's presumably different.

Let's turn from the political constraints to the other constraints which you mentioned earlier. How does a Secretary of State get enough resources for his service?

By persuading, arguing, cajoling, exploiting his political position, being a bloody nuisance in Cabinet. Above all by being persistent. Obviously success depends on a whole mixture of factors, a lot of them a matter of luck – your relations with the Chancellor; your standing in the Cabinet; the way the rest of the Cabinet feels towards the education service; whether you can exhaust your colleagues before they exhaust you. It's an endless tactical battle which requires determination, cunning and occasional unscrupulousness. In an ideal world it would all no doubt be settled by some omniscient central unit, but this is the way it happens in our crude democratic world. And of course it's a primary function of a Minister of any Department to be successful with the Treasury, and his officials will quite rightly judge him by how successful he is.†

Does the Secretary of State for Education take up such issues first with the Chancellor or, since that decision affects the level of spending elsewhere, is there machinery for collective decision making?

Well, first there's a lot of discussion at official level between the spending Departments and the Treasury, and how well you do in this depends partly on how able your finance officer is. I was extremely lucky in Education in this respect. Then there will be bilateral discussions between spending Ministers and the Chancellor. Finally all disagreed points would come to the Cabinet in a nightmarish and interminable series of meetings,

*See p. 52,
†See p. 79 for Boyle's comment in the same vein.

usually in July but at other times also if there was a special blitz such as there was in January 1968.*

Does not the Treasury have too many roles to play? It might be considered to be an impartial 'staff' Department – collating and advising Ministers on estimates put up by the spending Departments.† It is also concerned with decisions on the economy. There might, for example, be choices to be made between less taxation and more schools. The Treasury will have to impartially collate these demands *and* put forward the arguments of those concerned with preserving the tax base. It is also sometimes called 'the central organ of government' arbitrating, at the official level, between Departments.‡ Should not economic policy be separate from financial control if other policies are to be allowed to compete effectively with it?

You mention four roles which the Treasury has. I'm not quite clear about two of them – the 'impartial staff Department' and the 'central organ of government'. But of course it has the other two roles – fiscal policy (more or less taxes) and total public expenditure (more or fewer schools). What happens is that the Treasury puts up to the Cabinet once a year a proposal on total public expenditure – that it should go up by x per cent or y per cent. The Cabinet either accepts this or puts in a different figure. Then the second stage is the argument about how you divide up the x per cent. The third stage is the following Budget when the Chancellor must meet the implications of the public expenditure decisions for his tax policy. I don't see how you can possibly separate the taxation from the public expenditure aspect, if that's what you're suggesting.

A lot of coordination takes place through decision making on expenditure. But are there not also decisions, on social services and education, which are taken outside the financial framework of decisions on estimates and the PESC review.**

---

*See p. 145.
†This is the normally accepted role of financial control in most organizations.
‡See p. 38.   **Public Expenditure Survey Committee.

Generally, as I've said, Education is a pretty independent Department, not much subject to Cabinet or Cabinet Committees. But, of course, there are occasions when coordinated decisions are needed outside the public expenditure field. A good example is local government reorganization. This concerned Housing, Education, Health and many other services. We achieved this coordination by the normal method of inter-Departmental committee. On this occasion the Prime Minister set up a special Cabinet Committee of which I was the Chairman, called the Local Government Reorganization Committee. We held a large number of meetings, and discussed and decided such issues as whether education was to be a top- or lower-tier function in the metropolitan areas, and how it should be related to the other services. An official committee had, of course, done a mass of preparatory work, and on this occasion – unusually – we had officials sitting in on the Ministerial Committee to assist on points of detail. I think both the Ministerial and official Committees were particularly effective on this occasion. At any rate, the general answer is that coordination outside the public expenditure field is done through the regular machinery of inter-Departmental committees – either *ad hoc* committees or, more usually, the normal structure of Cabinet Committees. And of course a lot is settled at Cabinet Committees without having to go to the Cabinet.

Can we now turn to relations with the school system? What is the role of the central Department in relation to local education authorities and schools? Is it really the top of a managerial system, of a single organization with authority and accountability running through it?

No, you couldn't conceivably describe it in these terms – there is in no sense a single organization with a managerial chain of command. On the other hand I was very struck by how much influence, control, power, or whatever the right word is, the Department has. There are all the constraints that I mentioned earlier, yet despite them a Minister can have a huge influence on the system.

But let's change sides for a moment – were there not great

changes in the Department's role in the period that you worked there?

Yes. Before the 1944 Act the Board of Education was more concerned to hold the ring between the 'real' protagonists, the local authorities, churches and parents, than to exercise positive influence or control. Its functions were regulatory and quasi-judicial. It added planning and development functions in the late 1940s and 1950s when it created the Architects and Building Branch, the Teacher Supply Branch and so on. These were of course both concerned with the effective use of resources. It was with Eccles that the Department became increasingly concerned with the development of the educational system as such – further education, teacher training, comprehensivization, as well as the sadly misunderstood attempt to help the schools by creating the Curriculum Study Group.* By the time you came Ministers were able to take a lead on such hitherto untouchable subjects as the future of higher education – universities and all. Many people were and are frightened by the change from negative control to positive policy making.

I would certainly agree that the positive role was growing while I was there, and had grown, as you say, in the previous few years.

Do you think there is a growing public demand for central control of standards?

I don't know whether there's a *growing* public demand – after all, there's already considerable central control over standards, isn't there? School building standards as regulated by cost limits, for a start, and indeed the whole pace and size of the building programme. And the Department has a lot of influence, if not control, over pupil–teacher ratios through the teacher recruitment quotas as well as the flow of recruits to

*The Curriculum Study Group was set up by David Eccles in March 1962 with the job of 'foreseeing changes before they become apparent on the ground' (letter from the Permanent Secretary, Dame Mary Smieton, to LEAs and teachers' associations, which also described the Group as 'a significant change in the organization of the Ministry').

the colleges of education; over the size of classes in FE – it has to approve all advanced courses; indirectly over the staff–pupil ratio in universities; over access to higher education in different parts of the country; and so on. The Department's agreement is necessary to changes in salary scales. There's an endless flow of advice, exhortation and instruction through circulars, administrative memoranda and official and semi-official letters, and this must condition the standards provided by the local authorities. And generally, local government finance is strongly affected by the amount of rate-support grant allocated by the Secretary of State for the Environment for all local authority services, including education which is the largest spender.

What views did you develop about the relationship between the DES and local authorities?

All governments and Ministers are a bit schizophrenic about their relationship with local authorities. On the one hand they genuinely believe the ringing phrases they use about how local government should have more power and freedom, and that's why we all want local government reform. On the other hand a Labour government hates it when Tory councils pursue education or housing policies of which it disapproves, and exactly the same is true of a Tory government with Labour councils. This ambivalence exists in everybody I know who is concerned with relations between central and local government. In any event, until there's reorganization you can't give local authorities much more power than they have at the moment. They need to be stronger, larger, more efficient, to employ more technical and professional staff and the rest of it, before you could have any significant transfer of power.

But these are general remarks. As far as education is concerned I wasn't conscious at DES of any great problem or any demand on either side for a major change in our relationship with LEAs. The one exception was over comprehensive reorganization, and no doubt you'll want to come to that later. But generally we went out of our way to give as much freedom as possible – for example, on the age of transfer and on building programmes.

But individual head teachers are miles away from the Secretary of State. Does the Secretary of State have any real connection with what actually goes on in schools? Or does government concern itself with providing resources and ensuring that the authorities and schools give children and the public what they are entitled to have – while the real work goes on in the schools?

Well, the Secretary of State, as we've already agreed, has a very close connection with the number and quality of the teachers and with what the buildings are like. But I imagine you're referring to internal organization and curriculum. And here you're right that the only influence is the indirect one that is exercised through HMIs, through DES participation in the Schools Council and through government-sponsored research projects like the one on comprehensive education.* The nearer one comes to the *professional* content of education, the more indirect the Minister's influence is. And I'm sure this is right.

The essential processes of education within the school itself are largely impervious to any Departmental control. I wonder how this compares with other services?

I mistrust comparisons with other services – they're all so different in what they provide. For instance, Housing has its inspectorate – the Alkali Inspectorate – but their function is quite different from that of HMIs. But it's interesting that in the last year or so Health has been establishing something more akin to the HMI system.

Teachers have a considerable amount of freedom in what and how they teach. There is their growing professionalism and their aspirations about professionalism – for example the desire to have control over their own standards. How far is this an unattractive form of syndicalism or is it a good thing in its own right?

*A Schools Council for the Curriculum and Examinations was established in 1964 after recommendations by Sir John Lockwood's working party on this subject, which was set up by Edward Boyle in July 1963.

I would have thought that in principle it was a good thing –
provided there are central sources of advice and guidance
like HMIs, the Schools Council and the Institutes of Education.* I certainly don't think Ministers or civil servants are
competent to interfere in detail. True, I referred in one or two
speeches to the question of streaming. But generally I didn't
regard either myself or my officials as in the slightest degree
competent to interfere with the curriculum. We're educational
politicians and administrators, not professional educationalists.

How does a Minister and a Department get itself advised?
What about central and national advisory councils? For ex-
ample, what about the National Advisory Council for the
Training and Supply of Teachers?

I did not reappoint the NAC after its *Eleventh Report*, despite continuing protests, and I would never have done so. It
was concerned with the future supply and demand for teachers. I thought that was a job that should be done inside the
Department and not by an amorphous outside body. If the
Department couldn't do that job, which was central to all its
activities, it ought to pack up.

What about the CAC?†

Well, the Department didn't much like it, as you know better
than anyone else!‡ And you can see their point of view. The
reports got longer and longer, and more and more monu-
mental, and took up more and more of the time of already

*Institutes of Education are university-provided bodies (with the excep-
tion of Cambridge) which provide in-service and advanced training for
teachers as well as acting as the examining bodies for colleges of education.

†The Central Advisory Councils for Education (England and Wales) have
the duty to 'advise the Minister on such matters connected with educational
theory and practice as they think fit and upon any questions referred by him
to them', and have produced the Crowther, Newsom, Plowden reports etc.
(A critical survey of the major CAC reports is to be found in Anne Corbett,
Much To Do about Education, Council for Educational Advance, 1968.)

‡Maurice Kogan was Secretary to Lady Plowden's Central Advisory
Council. He only knew that 'the Department didn't like it' some time after
he was appointed.

hard-worked officials. Some of the reports were very good; others, like Newsom, could have been sharper – though the 'Newsom child' has been a most important and influential concept. Plowden did the same, brilliantly, with educational priority areas. I hadn't taken a final decision, but I think I would have reappointed it once more for a fairly quick inquiry into teacher training, and then sought a change of law enabling it to be disbanded as a permanent body.

But the CAC did document the good and the bad of the system and, in particular, legitimized the radical sociology of the 1950s and 1960s. It was done better than by any other single group of documents.

Yes, that's true, and a profoundly important point. But there's a danger of too many and too lengthy reports. And they can slow up action, as Plowden would have done on comprehensive reorganization if I hadn't been very firm. Anyway I think we've got to a point now where this general theme of education and social background – what you call the radical sociology – has been taken in and it doesn't need more inquiries to drive it home. We've got a large body now of active educationalists who can carry this discussion on themselves. The point of having outside committees should now be to inquire into more precise and specific issues.

But you still have to have independent critical intelligences at work on policy issues. Are you suggesting that the civil service and Ministers can fulfil this function themselves?

I'm sure they can't. I greatly felt the need for independent critical advice. But it wouldn't necessarily come from government committees. I had my own informal group of personal advisers, and of course by now there's a huge volume of critical writing on education, by which I don't mean partisan editorials in *The Times Educational Supplement* which was then wildly reactionary, but serious articles, books and journals.

What about the relationship between the Minister and his Department and the important pressure groups. For example,

Sir William Alexander must have been as well acquainted with Departmental thinking, and consulted about it, as any Deputy Secretary.* And similarly with the other local authority and teacher associations. Their officials are extremely experienced and long lived. They survive Ministers and Permanent Secretaries. What effect do they have on the process of policy making and decision making in the Department?

Certainly these are powerful bodies with able and influential officials, and one always had to try to carry them along. You can't in this country railroad policies through regardless of the views of local authorities and teachers, and you shouldn't try. Of course the Minister must take the final decision on basic issues of national policy – the priorities for spending, whether to go comprehensive, the binary system. But it's very important to try and go as far as you can by consultation and cooperation. If I take one example, I was greatly influenced by what the NUT said in my consultations with them on the draft of *Circular 10/65* about the need for local authorities genuinely to consult the teachers; and I was influenced by much that the AEC said about the draft. I think this produces a better result than the one Mrs Thatcher produced by rushing into print with *Circular 10/70* without any consultation of any kind.†

Both these national bodies contribute quite a bit to the policy making process. Year after year they comment on policies as they are made. They give evidence to the various bodies that are set up. Have they got continuity?

Yes, their role, amongst other things, is that of continually commenting on policy as it develops. Sometimes you accept their advice and sometimes you don't. The Association of Teachers in Technical Institutions, for example, had a lot of influence on the development of the binary policy. The minority report of the ninth NAC report on the supply and training of teachers was influential – it had a definite effect on the so-

---

*William Alexander is Secretary to the Association of Education Committees. See also pp. 134–5.

†For *Circular 10/70* see p. 52.

called productivity exercise.* And I always kept in very close touch with the officers of the national bodies. I would often, for example, meet Alexander and an informal group of Directors of Education, and I kept in close contact with the leaders of the teacher's organizations.

What about the other and more informal pressure groups – the Confederation for the Advancement of State Education or the Advisory Centre for Education, for example?

I think one of the most encouraging trends in the last few years has been the growth of an informed educational public opinion, manifested in bodies like CASE nationally and parents' associations locally. I've always been a very strong supporter of these bodies, and the fact that they were almost wholly pro-comprehensive was a major factor in the dynamic that we got behind *Circular 10/65* in the early years. Indeed we can see how that influence persists even now in the fact that Surrey and Richmond, for example, after years of opposition to the *10/65* policy, are now finally moving in the comprehensive direction even after Mrs Thatcher's withdrawal of *10/65*.

May we now turn to relations with civil servants? Is the popular assumption about bureaucratic obstructionism a fair one?

No, certainly not. It's very rare that you meet real resistance or obstruction. I can think of only a few instances. One was the creation of a Planning Branch.† Another was over the Council for Educational Technology which at that time seemed a major breakthrough and which the best people in the field greatly welcomed, but which was quite strongly opposed in the Department.‡

*National Advisory Council (England), *The Demand for and Supply of Teachers, 1963–1986*, Ninth Report, HMSO, 1965. Its Supplementary Minority Report proposed a four-term year for the colleges of education. Its signatories were either local authority representatives or the Secretary of State's nominated members.

†The DES Planning Branch was set up in 1966.

‡The National Council for Educational Technology was set up in March 1967 'to advise bodies concerned with education and with training in industry and the services on audio-visual aids and media and the most

Was the opposition based on technical grounds or were there established Departmental objectives which conflicted with policies you wanted to introduce?

I think in the case of the Planning Branch it was based partly on general conservatism and partly on administrative argument. The administrative argument was that a Department like Education didn't need a central planning division because the planning function was already being carried out in the separate operating branches – teacher supply, school building, further education, and so on. I didn't agree. On the Council for Educational Technology the resistance was due partly to a scepticism about what role it could play, partly to the intense dislike of outside councils and committees which all civil servants have and which I can understand, and partly to fears that the Council would lead to a level of expenditure which would make difficulties with the Treasury.

On another issue, the Public Schools Commission, there was a lot of very legitimate argument which I thought did great credit to the civil servants. They were sceptical as to whether the government knew what it was doing. They rightly challenged me on whether there was any possible compromise solution which a commission could recommend and which stood a chance of acceptance on both financial and political grounds. I insisted and got my way, and we set up the Commission. I must say that much of their scepticism eventually proved justified!

A Secretary of State has wide ranging responsibilities. Otherwise he would not need so many senior and able officials working for him. How can he possibly control all of this work? If he cannot, does his accountability for what he cannot control weigh heavily?

The answer is, he can't possibly control everything and shouldn't try. A Minister has to decide what to be interested in and what to delegate. The worst sort of Minister is the one who tries to control it all, and stays up till 3 a.m. each night

appropriate and economical ways of using them' (D E S, *Annual Report for 1967*, Cmnd. 3564).

going through endless red boxes and getting himself bogged down in detail. You must rigorously pick and choose the crucial subjects that you're going to concern yourself with.

But the price you pay for this is that occasionally you approve a decision that you haven't gone into yourself in detail and you find you're landed in a political mess. There are two occasions I can remember where I accepted a decision without sufficient study and landed myself in a mess. In both cases I think the decision was absolutely correct, but the whole presentation was frightful because the civil servants had not thought out what the reaction was likely to be. The first concerned the Welsh College of Advanced Technology. It was one of the few CATs that was not to become an independent university. We put it together with the University of Wales. But there was passionate local feeling that it should become a separate Cardiff University.* I have no doubt the decision was right, but we idiotically announced it in answer to a written question on the day before the House rose just before Christmas. This made the storm much worse because everybody in Wales thought we were trying to slip it through in an underhand way.

The other case was overseas students' fees, which also came up to me virtually on the last day of Parliament and was also announced in a written answer.† That created an even worse storm which we'd made no preparations to meet. The officials had either misjudged or else failed to warn me of the likely reaction in the universities, and the whole announcement and presentation were totally mishandled. But those are the only occasions I can remember when I was landed in a mess as a result of delegation – and even in these examples both issues were given to me for decision, though a bit too late in the day.

On the second point – does it all weigh heavily – no, not if you've got a good digestion. It's an inevitable fact of life. For

*The Welsh College of Advanced Technology became The University of Wales Institute of Science and Technology at Cardiff in 1967.

†*Education* (4 August 1967) said of the decision to charge overseas students higher fees than UK-resident students, 'Mr Crosland has clashed directly with some of the Vice-Chancellors ... over the overseas students' fees decision which showed him at his most high-handed and gave him his worst press.'

instance, in the Board of Trade hundreds of decisions are being taken each year on Industrial Development Certificates. I delegated these entirely to a junior Minister and officials and refused to look at them unless there was a violent disagreement on a major case between the junior Minister and the officials, which happened perhaps twice a year. But it doesn't weigh heavily, no, provided you sleep well and have a robust constitution.

You must feel that if you could give more of your time you would find things you had scarcely heard about? Somebody says 'The Minister had decided that ...' and you don't even know. Doesn't that keep you awake at night?

You would certainly find things you had scarcely heard of. For example, even after two years at the Board of Trade I had had no contact at all with the Patent Office and practically none with Weights and Measures. But I never lay awake at night thinking 'Gosh, I wonder what those chaps at the Patents Office are up to.' The only things that would keep you awake at night are sudden crises, and the likelihood of these varies enormously between Departments. Obviously they're liable to happen at any time in the Foreign Office. The Treasury's quite cushy from this point of view unless there's a violent run on sterling. Probably the worst Department is the Home Office, where the Minister is always liable to be rung up in the middle of the night over a foster-parent case, or a prisoner escaping from Dartmoor or a dramatic immigration case. Education wasn't like that at all – partly, I suppose, because the Department doesn't deal much with individual members of the public, it's the local authorities that do.

But you would be in favour of the British system then, that a Minister does have responsibility for all decisions?

Well, it doesn't worry me, and because it doesn't worry me I haven't thought deeply about it. I know some of my colleagues believe that civil servants should take more public responsibility, but I confess I haven't thought about this at all closely. The system has obviously loosened up a great deal. Civil servants now give public lectures and press interviews in a way they would never have done before, and that's obviously a good thing.

If one is lucky two hundred or maybe three hundred civil servants out of an administrative class of three thousand have something in them – a creative policy – that they want to see forwarded. And here again one comes to such figures as Morrell or Morant. At present, civil servants don't carry the can publicly. They don't get the incentive to be more imaginative and more openly creative than they are now, because everything they do is cannibalized by the system in one way or the other. Isn't one really wasting potential if civil servants are shielded from blame and required to remain anonymous if they make a valuable contribution? What sort of bureaucrats do we want?

There are two separate questions here. First, whether the present system gives sufficient outlet to the imaginative and creative civil servant. I believe that it does. I don't believe he is seriously inhibited under the present system. There was always a handful of civil servants in Curzon Street – one or two of them Deputy Secretaries now – who said what they believed with great logical and moral force and I, and I'm sure all other sensible Ministers, expected and wanted them to do so. They can't be named, it's true, but they, and their colleagues, and the upper reaches of the educational world would know whom I mean. They are anything but faceless in the world in which they work.

The second question is whether it matters that a civil servant is not publicly responsible for his own mistakes. Well, it's certainly true that his name doesn't get into the press, and he's spared that. But a really bad mistake is known all around Whitehall – the gossip that goes on is something absolutely out of this world. I once had some totally wrong advice on a highly technical subject, and as a result looked an absolute fool in Cabinet – the whole issue had to be postponed at great inconvenience. There was a quite formal inquiry in the Department on what had gone wrong, and the official responsible didn't recover for six months – he came near to a nervous breakdown, simply from the humiliation within the circuit.

So although there's no press publicity, there's a great deal of informal publicity within the official's own group. And people of course mind desperately about that.

But shouldn't credit or discredit be evident outside the closed world of Whitehall? The remarkable ones always take care of themselves. They would have been remarkable in any situation. But measure this against the number who are driving out quite major chunks of policy or decisions. Should they not be accountable for what they do publicly as well as accountable to their Minister and their own civil service chiefs? Might it not generate even better policies and good work?

You must remember what I've just said – that a high or low reputation often penetrates far outside the world of Whitehall. Civil servants in many Departments have an extremely wide clientele. In Education, an Under-Secretary – and his virtues or faults – will be well known to the university world, or the local authority world, or the teachers' organizations. In the Board of Trade an official will be highly or badly regarded in, say, the CBI, the British National Export Council, the textile industry or what you will. In other words his work and his quality will be known and judged over a wide field. And often, incidentally, it will be better judged than that of the politician, who may cover up his weaknesses by a slick and quick-witted performance in Parliament. So the civil servant's motivation is pretty strong. I still have to be convinced that we should improve matters by making him publicly accountable to Parliament and the press.

And that's quite apart from the desire for promotion, which of course is as strong in the civil service as anywhere else. There's probably still a bit too much promotion by seniority. But there's a great deal less than there used to be, and generally the system rewards the able. The procedures are scrupulously fair. All very senior promotions go to an inter-Departmental panel, and so are discussed by people outside the Department. The Prime Minister will take a close personal interest. So of course will the Departmental Minister. But he should only concern himself with senior appointments – in a large Department he simply won't have time to get to know all the junior officials well enough to have an accurate view of their relative merits. I always refused to interfere with any promotion below the level of Under-Secretary.

You probably can't answer this in detail, but was there any major issue that was put to you by officials that you turned down?

Yes, indeed there were such cases. But they're not all that numerous because civil servants usually have the sense not to put things up which they think will be turned down. They're busy men and don't want to waste their time. Generally I found it perfectly simple to establish good relations with civil servants – why shouldn't it be? One of the few times I ever had bad relations was when I first went to the Board of Trade and said I proposed to reopen the Stansted decision. I shall never forget the row of black faces! The officials thought they had finally got Stansted sown up, and were enraged to have the whole wretched matter reopened. They thought I was mad and wrong. My relations with that group of people were pretty bad for some time. But that was an unusual case because I was reopening a decision which it had taken them years of work to arrive at.

The most enjoyable relations I ever had with a group of officials was with the comprehensive reorganization team at Education. They were a lot of enthusiasts, young, bright, and with a remarkable *esprit de corps*. But generally I never found any problem in establishing good working relations. And a Minister who doesn't do so is wasting a large fund of knowledge and experience.

How many cases were there when you drew yourself up to your full Ministerial height and said 'This is a Ministerial decision'? Or does the process emerge as one of rational dialectic between the permanent experts and yourself, taking decisions as a result of rational discourse?

There were of course cases – Stansted at the Board of Trade was an obvious example – where I had to say 'this is now my decision', knowing that some or all of the officials were strongly against it. I tried to avoid making a great drama or confrontation out of it, because this method tends to humiliate people publicly and is bad for morale. But there's not the slightest difficulty in making your decisions clear in a perfectly tactful manner. You can do it in a meeting or in writing as you prefer. Over the Planning Branch, for example, I sent a polite minute to Herbert Andrew saying, 'I would be grateful for your final advice on this matter as I propose to make a public announcement in a fortnight's time.' An experienced civil servant can always tell when the argument is over and he's lost the battle. But of course there are many other cases where a decision emerges naturally from discussions between the Minister and his officials. The officials know what the government's broad policies are, and they tender advice in the light of them. It's a great mistake to think there's a continuous battle going on.

But can Ministers be run by civil servants?

Oh, certainly. One Minister I know simply read his Departmental brief out to the Cabinet. The whole thing was underlined in red ink and he simply read it out. Absolutely extraordinary. At the other extreme is the Minister who believes in getting his way by shouting. Andrew Duncan, Anthony Eden and Lord Woolton were all shouters.* So was George Brown in the Labour government, gifted man though he was. Of course the officials hate it, and so they should. You don't shout at people like this in other forms of life, and you've absolutely no need to in order to get your way.

Can Ministers really have a dialogue within the Department? The contributors are not on an equal footing and there must be tension between civil servants and Ministers?

There shouldn't be this tension if the Minister is a sensible and

*Sir Andrew Duncan (died 1952) was President of the Board of Trade in 1940 and 1941, and Minister of Supply 1940–41 and 1942–5. Sir Anthony Eden (now the Earl of Avon) was Lord Privy Seal 1934–5, Minister without Portfolio 1935, Secretary of State for Foreign Affairs 1935–8, for Dominion Affairs 1939–40, for War 1940, for Foreign Affairs 1940–45 and 1951–5, and Prime Minister 1955–7. Viscount Woolton (died 1964) was Minister of Food 1940–43, Minister of Reconstruction 1945, Lord President 1945 and 1951–2, and Chancellor of the Duchy of Lancaster 1952–7.

civilized person. On the contrary, a Minister who knows how to utilize his civil servants – and some Ministers conspicuously don't, they are too touchy and defensive – will acquire a strong feeling of camaraderie with the good ones amongst them. As to a dialogue, I never found the slightest difficulty in getting one, especially at Education. We had a sustained dialogue, for example, about the terms of reference of the Public Schools Commission. Nobody had an absolutely clear view and the senior officials were divided among themselves. There was another occasion, during the 1966 election, when I said that I wanted all Under-Secretaries and upwards to give me their views in writing on the age of transfer, and the result was a totally frank and extremely valuable exchange of views. Curzon Street was a very unstuffy place – officials didn't object to their juniors expressing contrary views. I see no problem at all about getting a dialogue within a Department. Of course you don't treat all your officials as if *they* were on an equal footing amongst themselves. You discover fairly early on that some are good and some are bad, so you listen to the good ones and don't listen to the bad ones. If you've got any sense you will ask your predecessor his views on the officials – though it's incredible how rarely this is done. Soon after I went to Curzon Street I had a long talk with Edward Boyle about all the senior civil servants, but neither of my successors there ever asked me for my views. But you soon discover from the files coming up to you which are the able ones and which the pedestrian ones. You can't conceal mediocrity very easily. Any intelligent Minister reading a file can quickly see if he's getting competent advice.

Where do outsiders fit in? What precisely would you expect the outsider, presumably the well-qualified outsider, to do within the Department? Would he be advising you directly, but not taking decisions himself? What would be his role?

I think we have to break this question down. There are three sorts of outside advice which you want – or at any rate which I want – in addition to the Departmental advice. First, there's the *professional* expert – the economist, the sociologist, the scientist, or whatever. As an ex-economist, I was particularly keen on economics. I brought Ian Byatt into Education, and also Chelly Halsey as a sociologist. And at the Board of Trade I brought in Wilfred Beckerman, John Wright and Alan Day, Their function was to advise both myself and the regular officials, not of course to take decisions It seems incredible, but when I went to Education there wasn't an economist there at all, and only a single senior one even at the Board of Trade.

Secondly, I wanted independent *educational* advice as a check on the advice I was getting from the Department. But I wanted it from people whose sympathies were Labour. So I had two groups of people, one for schools and one for higher education, who used to meet periodically in my house. They were people like John Vaizey, Michael Young, Noel Annan, Asa Briggs, David Donnison and so on; and once or twice I invited Herbert Andrew to come. I suppose they were mostly academics. But the discussion was very unacademic. I would say that I want tonight to discuss the binary system or university accountability or the age of transfer. The agenda was always concerned with matters where a decision was required. There was no general chatter – and they got no drinks until the serious discussion was over. People become much too talkative if you give them something to drink.

Lastly, you want straight *political* advice. Ideally you get this from your junior Ministers. But they can be a very mixed bunch in terms of temperament and political outlook, and meetings with all the junior Ministers, which sounds the obvious way of going about things, were always rather a shambles, with one person talking too much of the time. So in fact you talk to them separately. And if you've got the sense, and the luck, to find a good PPS or two good PPSs then they can play an invaluable role in keeping you in touch with party feeling. I was very lucky at Education in having Chris Price and Bob Mitchell as PPSs. Both were extremely helpful on comprehensive schemes in particular and on educational politics generally.

You were advised by outsiders as experts, or at least some of them as experts. Could you now comment on the expertise of the civil servants? Did you find them amateurs, or was there sufficient expertise for you to do the work properly with their help?

Well, it would be ridiculous for me to describe them as amateurs, having myself spent only two-and-a-half years as Education Minister. They were certainly much more expert than I was. I think they were all professional education administrators with a lot of knowledge and expertise, depending mainly on how long they had been in the Department. The distinction wasn't between amateur and professional, but according to how long or short a time they had been there and whether they were able or not.

Common to the general lot of humanity.

Quite. I never distinguished between amateur and professional in Education. They were professional administrators. When people speak of civil servants being amateurs, they tend to think of the arts graduate in the Treasury who has had no training of any kind in economics. And certainly, when I went to the Board of Trade I felt that, rusty as I was, I still knew more about economics than most of the senior administrators. But I don't think you can argue by analogy from this to Education. You're surely not suggesting that all civil servants at Curzon Street should have degrees in education! That wouldn't make them any better at getting more teachers or building more schools.

Could I make a point on this? They were expert on the law of administration, on the financial system, on the systems of rights and duties. But the Department was backward for an awful long while, on the new information that was developing in sociology, educational psychology and the rest. It wasn't the Department, in fact, that cracked the 11-plus doctrine, but it was mainly such outsiders as Vaizey, Floud, Halsey and the rest.

I hesitate to comment on that, as when I got there it was of course settled policy to get rid of the 11-plus. I suppose it's a general truth that new ideas and intellectual breakthroughs normally come from the outside academics – that happens in every field, although you yourself earlier mentioned people like Morant and Morrell as being innovators. Academics are paid to have new ideas, civil servants are paid to administer. But I should have thought that the brighter officials, at any rate, would keep up with the academic work in their spare time and would be pretty well aware of what was going on.

What Can a Secretary of State Achieve?

Given the contraints and relationships within which a Minister works, what were the highlights of your period in office, what can a Minister actually do?

It's really harder for me to answer that than it would be for an objective critic. But trying to be as honestly introspective as I can, I think my answer would be as follows. I think that the prime achievement was a matter of morale and impetus. A Minister has the duty – indeed he alone can fulfil this duty – of trying to create a sense of impetus, of things moving, of deep concern for education, a sense that we are all actively working towards the goal of better education, a sense of positive partnership between government, local authorities and teachers. The educational world needs to feel that the people in Curzon Street really care and are working furiously to push things forward. This is partly a matter of one's relationships with the local authorities and the teachers' organizations and so on, of giving the impression of wanting a constructive dialogue with them, of wanting to hear their views, of sharing certain common objectives. And it's partly a matter of using the platform that only a Minister has to create a strong sense of impetus and leadership. A Minister, unlike any of his officials, has a Parliamentary platform, he has the platform provided by the major educational events of the year, such as the NUT Conference and the AEC Conference, and he has the platform provided by having to meet numerous deputations from all the organizations in the educational world. He also has access to the press, and again should use this to create the feeling that things are happening and something is moving, and that we all passionately want a better educational system and that there are a lot of people everywhere working enormously hard to achieve this. And I would like to think, although, as I say, this is more for a critic to judge than for me, that while I was there we succeeded in creating this sense of movement and impetus, so contributing to a higher morale in the whole service.

Perhaps we can take a number of the most important policies in education to see who had a say in them and what was your role? Let's start with *Circular 10/65*.

Yes. The basic policy of going comprehensive was, of course, decided before I got there. It was in the Labour Party's election manifesto, and the decision to issue a circular had been made by Michael Stewart before I arrived. My role was to influence the form, the content and the style of the circular, subsequently to take the basic tactical decisions on individual cases like Liverpool and Luton, and generally to set the mood and determine the strategy of the operation.

Subsequently there was some criticism that you could have two different local authorities both operating 10/65 and yet for the individual child there would be very different patterns. How did that arise? Could you say how you arrived, or why you arrived, at six optional schemes? Was this you, or the HMIs, or who?

There's no question but that we had to have options. For one thing, the legacy of existing buildings compelled it – it meant, for example, that a lot of areas *had* to have a two-tier system. And secondly there was no clear consensus on which type of organization was best on merit – all-through comprehensives, or the Leicestershire system, or what.* So there was no alternative to allowing options. The detail of the options was mainly a product of thinking in the Inspectorate.

Here we have HM Inspectors giving technical advice on something you thought politically desirable.

*See DES *Circular 10/65*, where 'all-through school' is defined as 'the orthodox comprehensive' with an age range of eleven to eighteen. The Leicestershire system – also known as the Mason system after S. C. Mason, Director of Education for Leicestershire – was started, experimentally, in 1957. It is an 'end on' two-tier system whereby all pupils on leaving primary school transfer to a junior comprehensive. At the age of thirteen or fourteen some pupils move on to a senior school while the remainder stay on in the same school.

Certainly.

Once policy was decided what did you have to go through to get this process moving forward? The circular was already sorted out in principle before you got there. How did you negotiate this with local authorities, teachers' associations, and what was this process like?

The circular existed in embryo form when I got there. I thought it was pretty unreadable and full of officialese, so I did what I always have done with major documents – a great deal of redrafting of the language to try and create the kind of document that I wanted. At the same time discussion was still going on about points of substance, in particular about the various options. Then the draft went out to all the associations. They made written comments and I had long meetings with all the main bodies. There's no doubt that the consultation was real and genuine. In fact the internal discussion and outside consultation took months and months – I arrived at Curzon Street in January and the circular didn't finally go out until July.

You have described how the circular was drafted, after a great deal of internal consultation within the Department; you have also said that there was a lot of consultation with the outside educatioral and teachers' representative bodies. How far did these external consultations affect the content of the circular?

They didn't of course affect the basic principles, which were established Ministerial policy. But they did influence me on a number of important points. Let me give you some examples. First, there was a lot of argument inside the Department about whether we should 'request' or 'require' local authorities to produce comprehensive plans. Reg Prentice wanted 'require', the Department wanted 'request'.* My decision to go for 'request' was strongly influenced by my meetings with the AEC and my judgement of the general mood of the local authority world. Secondly, the very firm wording of

*Reginald Prentice was a Minister of State at the DES, October 1964 – January 1967, when he became Minister for Overseas Development.

paragraph 14, which made it clear that two-tier systems with optional transfer to a senior school were acceptable only for a transitional period – this was the product of intense discussion in the Department and with outside bodies. Thirdly, the section on consultation with the teachers was greatly strengthened as a result of discussions with the NUT, the NAS and the Joint Four, and no doubt the other teachers' organizations as well.* And fourthly, the paragraph on keeping parents fully informed was put in after meeting the Confederation for the Advancement of State Education.

One of the questions raised at the time was 'why not some research on this circular'? On the face of it, here was a major change, but the government had done no research on the effects.

Well, this argument had a natural attraction for an ex-academic like myself. But as soon as I thought the thing through I could see it was wrong. It implied that research can tell you what your objectives ought to be. But it can't. Our belief in comprehensive reorganization was a product of fundamental value-judgements about equity and equal opportunity and social division as well as about education. Research can help you to achieve your objectives, and I did in fact set going a large research project, against strong opposition from all kinds of people, to assess and monitor the process of going comprehensive. But research can't tell you whether you should go comprehensive or not – that's a basic value-judgement. In any case you have to remember that we weren't starting completely *tabula rasa*. The Swedes had been going at it for some time, and I got Professor Husén to come to Curzon Street and talk to us all.† He was wholly in favour of our pushing on as we were doing. And of course we had a number of compre-

*The NAS is the National Association of Schoolmasters. The 'Joint Four' refers to the Joint Committee of the Four Secondary Associations (i.e. Association of Headmistresses Incorporated, Incorporated Association of Headmasters, Association of Assistant Mistresses Incorporated, Incorporated Association of Assistant Masters.)

†Professor Torsten Husén is a leading Swedish educationalist – see his *School Reform in Sweden*, United States Office of Education, Division of International Education, 1961.

hensive systems here that had been going for quite a considerable time – in London and Leicestershire and elsewhere. In
fact 12 per cent of our children were already in comprehensive schools in 1965. And on top of that we had the whole
series of studies and reports – *Early Leaving*, J. W. B. Douglas,
Crowther, Newsom – which showed the effect of selection on
children's chances. I thought it was right (and this was the
first time I think it was done in this country), having decided on the objective, to have research to monitor the process
to see what we could learn as we went along. But there was
no conceivable case for holding up the circular for another
three years until some further bit of research had been done.

*Do you regret now not taking statutory power to get it through
at that time?*

No. You must remember that at that time most local authorities were Labour-controlled and sympathetic to what we were
doing – as indeed were some Tory authorities. So plans were
coming in at least as fast as we could cope with them. For the
whole time I was at Curzon Street the thing was going as fast
as it could possibly go. The limitation was one of human and
physical resources and not one of statutory powers. But of
course the situation changed later when the disastrous local
election results of 1968 and 1969 put the Tories into power
almost everywhere.

*Could we now discuss teacher supply and your famous speech
outlining fourteen ways of producing and utilizing teacher
manpower more efficiently?* *

*The speech was made to the Annual Conference of the N U T in April
1965. The fourteen points were as follows: 1. Colleges of education were
encouraged to use existing accommodation to the full, to increase the intake
of students and 2. Establish annexes to Colleges – the 'outposts'. 3. Colleges
of further education were urged to assist in teacher training. 4. It was
proposed to establish four or five more day Colleges. 5. The government
pledged to begin recruitment campaigns for married women, including a
national register of women who had left teaching. 6. A Working Party was
promised to consider ways of encouraging part-time teachers by allowing
pension rights, for example. 7. Local authorities were urged to set up more
nurseries. 8. Research was to be undertaken into ways in which part-timers
could be used. 9. There was to be a new initiative in providing refresher courses

None of the fourteen points were new in themselves. But the decision to have a fourteen-point plan and to give it top priority and generally to dramatize the situation produced, I think, a new sense of urgency. I didn't invent any of the fourteen points but perhaps I increased the impetus. We put an enormous drive first into the intensive use of the colleges – the so-called 20 per cent productivity exercise. Then secondly we had a strong push on everything that would bring in mature students, particularly day colleges and outposts. And thirdly we stepped up the pressure for married women returners, and on local authorities to accept far more part-time teachers. This was perhaps the greatest achievement of those years – to bring the problem of teacher supply within sight of solution.

It is particularly interesting that you regard it as one of the major achievements because on the face of it these ideas came from within the Department and were there well before you came. The distinctive contribution of the Secretary of State was to decide to push them forward and take them to the forcing point. You had to sell this to the system. Why does the Secretary of State have to push so hard?

I suppose because we live in an extremely conservative world. It's a world in which push does matter, and Ministers can push where others can't. Outposts, for example – I take great pride in this achievement. They are not the end of the world, but all the same quite a lot of extra teachers resulted. And in my own constituency, where I got one off the ground, it was an oddly important social achievement; it became something in

---

and courses of training for graduates. 10. A circular was sent to LEAs for comment on existing use of part-timers. 11. It was proposed that technical colleges could run training courses for teachers. 12. Part-time courses were proposed to suit the housewife and worker with free evenings and weekends. 14. A four-term year was suggested as recommended by the NAC report. Arguments were also put forward for the greater use of ancillary help i.e. secretarial, clerical, the care of sick children, playground supervision etc., including (controversially) help in the classroom from non-professional personnel.

the life of the community as well as producing more teachers. But I must add that the Under-Secretary then in charge of teacher supply deserves much of the credit for all this.

What was your role in establishing the binary system of higher education?

Well, I began by making an appalling blunder, from which I learnt a lesson I shall never forget. I got the whole thing off on the wrong foot by breaking my own rule. I said to the press when I first went to Curzon Street that I wouldn't make any pronouncements on major policy for the first six months, and I broke the rule by making the Woolwich speech. I think, looking back, that officials should not have advised me to make a major speech on the subject at that time. But of course the ultimate fault was mine for accepting the advice. I then had only a superficial knowledge of the subject, and every change I made in the draft of the speech made it worse. Incredible. It came out in a manner calculated to infuriate almost everybody you can think of, and in public relations terms it did considerable harm to the policy. The more I thought about it subsequently, the more I became utterly convinced that the policy was right; and I set out the real arguments for it in a most careful later speech at Lancaster. But the Woolwich speech put people's backs up quite unnecessarily, and I had to fight the policy through against a great deal of very strong opposition, including some in the Labour party.

Then were you bounced by officials into making the Wool-wich speech?

Well, I think they shouldn't have suggested to me that I made it, and I shouldn't have accepted the suggestion. They should have said: 'Look, Minister, this is a wildly complicated and controversial subject – we suggest you take three months to master it and make up your own mind about it. It's a bore you have to make a speech at Woolwich without talking about it, but you can always just say nice things about Quintin Hogg's father who founded the Woolwich Polytechnic.'

But they wanted to get the policy on the record as soon as

possible. They presumably looked at my diary for some time ahead, and saw that this couldn't be done at the NUT, and the AEC was probably a bit too late in the year, and there wasn't another obvious occasion for doing it. And I not only accepted the advice, but made the mistake of adding things to the speech which made it much more unpalatable. Of course the ultimate fault was mine. It's not a mistake I shall make again, to make a major speech on a subject which I don't fully understand. But, as I've said, when I finally mastered the subject I became a passionate believer in binary and poly-technics and I suppose did as much as anyone else to push the policy through.

The policy could be attacked from two completely different points of view, either the elitist point of view or the egalitarian point of view. Presumably the egalitarians hoped to make the non-university parts of higher education strong by merging them with the universities.

I'm not much concerned with the elitist attack, as I myself am a confirmed egalitarian. But the egalitarians who attacked the policy were wrong from two points of view. First, they drew a false analogy. They said that if you were against the 11-plus, you should be against an 18-plus. But at 11-plus an entire age group is moving up into a different stage of education, and the question is whether it does so in a selective or a non-selective fashion. At 18-plus nothing of the sort is happening. Most of the age group is not going on to higher education anyway, and, alas, will not do so for a long time to come. And of those who are going on, not all want a university type of education. Both the demand and the need is for a pluralist, not a unitary, system of higher education, and for alternative institutions which offer something totally different from the traditional universities.

The second fallacy was to believe that if you changed the organizational set-up from a binary to a unitary one, all the technical colleges would instantly achieve university standards of buildings, student residences, libraries, research, and so on. But quite apart from whether or not this would be a sensible policy, it wouldn't depend on the organizational structure, but on the total amount of money available and how this was distributed between the hundreds of different institutions in higher and further education.

But the first point is the crucial one. Tyrrell Burgess has put the case better than anyone else in his various writings – the need for institutions which cater not only for the traditional full-time degree courses, but for the part-time student, the sub-degree course, and the kind of education which has its roots in the technical college tradition.

It's interesting that this sort of change can be achieved in the further education system, if not smoothly, then quite decisively. There is a marked difference here between further education and schools: the controls are stronger from the centre and more decisive.

Yes, I agree the government's controls are strong here. We could lay down that we would follow a binary policy, choose the polytechnics, and say broadly what sort of courses they should follow.

How far could you have made a similar speech to the Woolwich speech – controversial and fundamental – about the universities? Could you have confronted the Department, not with a topical issue like a little bit more productivity, but saying 'Look, the party is going to have a big showdown with the universities'?

It's an academic question, because the universities were not in a position anyway to give us what we needed. First, they were in the throes of their post-Robbins expansion, and they couldn't possibly have given us the yet further expansion of numbers that we needed. Possibly a showdown could have pushed them a bit further in two to three years – though I'm not sure even of that in the light of their reaction last year to the twelve ways suggested by the DES of increasing throughput – but that would have been a quite unacceptable loss of time. Secondly, for reasons I've just given, the urgent need was for an expansion of polytechnic-style rather than university-style higher education.

Was there nevertheless a change in climate in the relationship between government and the universities while you were in office?

Yes, a clear change. We rejected the notion of having two Permanent Secretaries in the Department, one specially to look after the universities. Then I insisted that the universities should be made accountable to the PAC.* Lastly, and most important, the UGC itself was persuaded to take a much more positive line on productivity, specialization, concentration of subjects and control of building through cost limits. The type of letter reaching the universities from the University Grants Committee is now much more detailed in its guidelines for expansion.

What happened about public schools?

The Labour Party manifesto committed us to setting up a Commission. My role was to write the terms of reference, which were quite unusually long and detailed, and to choose the Chairman and the members.

When you set up the Commission did you really think it was going to come up with anything? Or did you regard it as a political move?

It was a political move in the perfectly proper sense that we were committed to it by our manifesto. There was also a good deal of pressure from the Parliamentary Labour Party. But of course it was more than that. I was convinced that we had to discover once and for all whether any compromise solution was practicable. By a 'compromise' solution I mean one that avoids the two extremes, one extreme being to 'abolish' the schools, whatever that means, the other being in effect to do nothing – just let in a handful of state pupils and fiddle around a bit with the tax concessions. I was convinced that we did not know what on earth a compromise scheme might look like, because nobody had ever looked in detail at the number of schools, their precise type and size, whether they could fit into

*This classic controversy is recorded in Public Accounts Committee, Session 1966–7, Special Report, *Parliament and the Control of Public Expenditure*, HC 290 of 1966–7.

a comprehensive system, what different kinds of entry might be possible, and so on. We were not competent to do this work in the Department because there was too much other work going on. The sensible thing was to set up a Commission to do it. They certainly produced a detailed scheme, but unfortunately nobody much liked it!

So it still really remains that it is a question of feasibility? In principle one should do something about them, and the plan is still there?

The scheme is still there, yes. There are two difficulties about it. The first is that it would cost a lot of money, and while you've still got slum schools and so on it's difficult to argue that this should have a top priority. Secondly, a lot of people in my party thought the scheme still left the schools in a fundamentally elitist position. The problem is still there and we shall eventually have to come back to it.

How did you begin to process the Plowden recommendations?

We set up a special working group inside the Department to go through all the recommendations in minute detail, but their work wasn't finished by the time I left. As you know, I made a rather anodyne speech in the House of Commons welcoming the report when it came out, and later a speech to the NUT – my last NUT speech – accepting certain parts of the report on the management of schools and things like that. I had a lot of work going on inside the Department and it was one of the things which I was coming back to in the autumn of 1967, had I returned to Curzon Street and not gone to the Board of Trade. I intended to make a major statement on the report as a whole in the autumn of 1967. But one major thing we had already done, and that was to get the principle of educational priority areas accepted and to get an extra £16 million for them. It was almost the last thing I did at Education and one of the things that gave me most satisfaction.

The DES has some perennial problems like school building. What impact did you have on it?

I thought the School Building Branch was one of the best run bits of the Department, and English school building was of course admired all over the world. But the Branch and I both thought that we could improve the procedures still further. So in a speech to the AEC in June 1966, I announced a whole package of administrative changes. We made the boundary between major and minor building programmes much more flexible. We established a substantial reserve of money so that authorities which pushed ahead fast could apply for a larger allocation. I announced lump sum allocations for the raising of the school-leaving age. I tried to give a further impetus to consortium building and generally to streamline the procedures. The point of a speech like that – and this is part of the role of a Minister – is that it concentrates thinking in the Department. You say you want to make a major speech on the building programme on such-and-such a date, and that you intend to announce a series of improvements. This forces the Department to bring out all the improvements they've wanted to make but somehow haven't got around to. You add a few extra ones and push the officials a bit further. And as a result a more systematic policy emerges more quickly than would otherwise be the case.

Were there other good examples of how the Secretary of State can stimulate change?

Well, I would like to think there were quite a lot of others, but I mustn't give an exaggerated impression. But to take one small example, an active Minister can have a big effect on the type of appointments that are made to various bodies. At the Board of Trade the average age of such appointments seemed to be about seventy-five! One instance at Education was that I was able to get Brian Flowers as Chairman of the Science Research Council.* He was my first choice but we'd run into difficulties. The Department had given up, but I said we must have him and we got him.

*Professor Sir Brian Flowers, Langworthy Professor of Physics, University of Manchester, has been Chairman of the Science Research Council since 1967.

This is a record of a lot of change in two or three years. But it does not cover all of the most important work of the Department. Special services, for example, teachers' pensions, go on without you knowing anything about them until there is a major change of legislation. Pensions dominated Eccles's and Vosper's lives for about a year, and you may not hear of them again until the Government Actuary comes up with something again twenty years later or one of the associations begins to grumble?*

That's absolutely true. A large part of any Department's work, which doesn't at that moment raise acutely controversial issues, will go on without the Minister being involved at all. I instanced patents and weights and measures at the Board of Trade. When I was Minister, I selected what seemed to me to be the crucial issues.

*D. F. Vosper (Lord Runcorn, died 1968) was Parliamentary Secretary, for part of the time under David Eccles, from 1954 to 1959 at the Ministry of Education.

Index

Accountant-General, 82, 123, 124

Adjournment debates, 87, 157

Administrative memoranda, DES, 171

Advisory Centre for Education, 176

Age of transfer, 171, 184, 185

Agriculture, Ministry of, comparison with DES, 34, 85, 142

Alexander, Andrew, 120

Alexander, William, 45, 97, 134–6, 175, 176

Allen, Douglas, 99

Anderson Committee (students' awards), 68

Andrew, Herbert, 52, 106, 138, 139, 158, 183, 185

Annan, Noel, 185

Apartheid, 84, 109, 142

Appointments to committees, 147

Architects and Building Branch, DES, 29, 170

Asquith, Herbert, 36

Assistant Secretaries, 73, 150

Association of Education Committees (AEC), 45, 66, 94, 134, 135, 156, 175, 187, 189, 194, 198

Association of Municipal Corporations (AMC), 134

Association of Teachers in Technical Institutions, (ATTI), 147, 175

Ayer, A. J., 47, 72, 133

Balance of payments, 145

Baldwin, Stanley, 108, 159

Balfour, Arthur, 150

Balogh, Thomas, 44

Bantock, S. H., 58, 91, 92

Beckerman, Wilfred, 185

Bernstein, Basil, 24, 130

Bevan, Aneuran, 17, 58

Beveridge, William, 149

Beveridge Report, impact on Boyle, 69

Bevin, Ernest, 22

Binary system, 52, 128, 147, 175, 185, 193–5

Birch, Nigel, 50

Black Papers, 14, 47, 123

Blaug, Mark, 21

Boothby, Robert, 72

Boyd-Carpenter, John, 104, 106

Briault, Eric, 136

Briggs, Asa, 185

BBC, and educational ideology, 22

Brown, George, 44, 123, 183

Budget (1963), 65

Building programmes, 171, 172

Bureaucracy, 84, 176

Burgess, Tyrrell, 46, 143, 195

Burke, Edmund, 17, 79

Burnham Committee, 26, 57, 68, 95

Butler, R. A., 25, 90

Byatt, Ian, 185

Cabinet, role of, 34–9, 89, 96, 97, 102, 109, 110, 111, 160, 161–3, 165, 167

collective responsibility of, 37, 38, 111

Haldane's definition of, 37, 98, 109, 111, 161, 163

Cabinet Committees, 95, 156, 161, 169
  Economic Policy, 95, 97
  Home Affairs, 95, 97
  on *Maud Report*, 37, 169
  on Rhodesia, 97
  on teacher supply, 81
Cabinet Office, 32, 108, 111–12
Capability Unit, 32, 38, 43, 163–4
Central Advisory Council for Education (C A C), 24, 53, 66, 131, 132, 173
  see also Crowther, *Early Leaving*, Newsom, Plowden
Central government
  relations with local authorities, 33–4
  reorganization, White Paper (1971), 32
Certificate of Secondary Education, 139
Chancellor of Exchequer, 70, 85, 86, 167
Chataway, Christopher, 46, 86, 97, 122, 123
Chief Policy Adviser, 114, 115, *see also* Fulton Committee report
Children and Young Persons' Act (1969), 29
Children's Department, Home Office, 29
Churches, and education, 170
Churchill, Winston, 13, 35, 53
Circulars, D E S, 171
Circular 10/65, *Circular 10/70*
  see Secondary education
Civil servants
  career prospects, 15, 150
  relations with Ministers, 39–44, 137–43, 150–51, 154, 176–87
Civil Service Department, 38
'Clause Four', 19
Clegg, Alec, 46, 136
Cockerill, G. F., 99
Colleges of advanced technology (CATs), 88, 113, 114, 125

Colleges of education, 128, 192
Common Market, 65, 95, 96, 98
Comprehensive schools, 170, 175, 188, 189, 191
  and Boyle's policy, 19, 115–16
  and Crosland's and Stewart's policy, 41, 146, 150, 152, 165, 174, 189
  N F E R research on, 146, 172
  see also Secondary education
Comptroller and Auditor-General, 147
Compulsory purchase, 55
Confederation for the Advancement of State Education (CASE), 45, 59, 133, 176, 190
Confederation of British Industry, 181
Conservative Central Office, 45, 89
Conservative Enemy, The, 18, 51, 149, 152
Conservative Party Conferences
  1962, 89, 90
  1968, 18, 45
Conservative Research Department, 118
Cooperative Independent Commission Report, 149
Corbett, Anne, 46, 173
County Councils Association, 134
Cowen, Noel, 93
Crankshaw, Edward, 75
Crosland, S. (Susan Barnes), 13, 155
Crossman, Richard, 12, 44
Crowther, Geoffrey, 47
Crowther Report (*15 to 18*), 21, 24, 81, 93, 138, 143, 191
Curriculum
  control of, 20, 26, 132, 172
  development, and Boyle, 57
Curriculum Study Group, 45, 66, 115, 170

Daily Telegraph, and Boyle, 19

Dalton, Hugh, 44, 79, 154
Day, Alan, 185
Defence policy, 164
De Gaulle, Charles, 65
Denominational schools, 26
Department of Education and
    Science (DES)
  Architects and Buildings
    Branch, 29
  Information Division, 46
  Minister's duties, 25
  relations with local authorities,
    26–31
  and Schools Council, 172
  style of administration, 27–9, 40
  Teacher Supply Branch, 29
Deputy Secretaries, 83, 180
Devaluation, 145
Donnison, David, 47, 52, 133, 185
Douglas, J. W. B., 191
Dow, Christopher, 110
Du Cann, Edward, 46, 122
Duncan, Andrew, 183

Early Leaving (CAC Report),
    24, 191
Easton, David, 133
Eccles, David, 17, 20, 22, 33, 35,
    46, 47, 53, 74, 83, 85, 88, 90,
    100, 118, 132, 137, 143, 162,
    170, 199
Economic Affairs, Department
    of, 145, 160, 162
Economic problems
    1962–4, 65 1964–7, 145–6
Economics of education, 20–21
Economic policy, 163, 164
Economists in government, 46,
    184, 185
Eden, Anthony (Lord Avon),
    53, 54, 183
Education, 28, 49, 134
Education Act (1944), 23
Education Act (1964), 78
Educational priority areas, 53,
    58, 90, 197
Educational psychology, 20, 28,
    29

Educational Reconstruction
    (White Paper, 1943), 26
Egalitarianism, 29, 194
'Eighteen-plus', 194
Elementary schools, 28
Eleven-plus exams, DES
    attitude towards, 28
  see also Selection in education
Elitism, 194
Embling, J. F., 73, 86
Employment White Paper (1944),
    69
English, Cyril, 131
Environment, Secretary of State
    for the, 171
Equality, 29, 164
  Boyle's discussion of, 129
  Crosland's definitions of, 23, 29,
    51, 92
Etatism, 25
Expenditure on education, 68

Fairlie, Henry, 54
Financial Times, 123
Flemming, Gilbert, 83
Floud, Jean, 24, 46, 91, 92, 186
Foreign affairs, 108
Foreign Office, 179
Fulton Committee report, 38, 114
Further education
  branches, DES, 83, 177
  demand for, 21
  establishment of system, 24
  Ministers' interest in, 48, 170
  White Paper on (1956), 20, 88
  see also Technical colleges
Future of Socialism, The, 149, 152

General Certificate of Education
    (GCE), 83, 84
General Elections,
    1964, 43, 67, 69, 76, 78, 79
    1966, 20, 184
    1970, 151
Gittins Committee and *Report*,
    147
Gordon Walker, Patrick, 35, 36,
    152

Gould, Ronald, 45, 97, 136
Grammar schools
  free places, 24
  number of places, 83, 84
Greenland, Tony, 118

Hadow Reports, 21, 42
Hailsham, Lord (Quintin Hogg),
  31, 55, 67, 90, 93, 106, 139, 193
Haldane Reports see Cabinet
Hall, Robert, 114
Halsey, A. H. (Chelly), 19, 20,
  24, 46, 91, 92, 166, 185
Handicapped, education of, 48
Hardie, Keir, 17
Head teachers, 172
Healey, Denis, 12, 77, 159
Health and Social Security,
  Secretary of State for, 117, 118
  Inspectorate, 172
Health service, 125
Heath, Edward, 12, 95, 105
Henderson, Arthur, 44, 79, 154
Henderson, Peter, 19, 67
Herbert Commission and *Report*,
  27
H M Is, 28, 29, 40, 50, 130, 173,
  188
Hertfordshire, 29, 127
Higher education
  demand for, 21, 102, 106, 152,
  171
  organization of, 105–7, 128, 158
  see also Robbins Report
Hoare, Samuel (Lord
  Templewood), 55–6, 87
Home, Alec Douglas-, 90, 97
  decision on two Ministers, 35, 71
  and middle schools, 35, 71
  on Robbins, 92, 93, 107
Home Office, 29, 69, 179
Hornsby, Richard, 17
Horsburgh, Florence, 35
Hospital service, 32–4, 58
Housing
  and Macmillan, 90
  policy, 163, 164

Housing and Local Government,
  Ministry of, 162
  Alkali Inspectorate, 172
Hudson, John, 29
Hume, David, 17, 18, 19
Husén, Torsten, 23, 92, 190

Immigrants (*Circular 7/65*), 146
Industrial Development
  Certificates, 179
Industrial Reorganization
  Corporation, 145
Industrial Training Bill, 87
I L E A, appointment of leader,
  46, 122 *see also* Chataway,
  Christopher
Institutes of Education, 173
I Q, testing, 23 *see also* Selection
  in education
International Monetary Fund
  credit, 66
Isserlis, A., 100

James, Eric (Lord), 106, 129
Jay, Douglas, 52
Jenkins, Roy, 12
Jennings, Ivor, 24, 61
Johnson-Marshall, Stirrat, 29
'Joint Four', 190
Joseph, Keith, 71

Kaldor, N., 149
Kogan, Maurice, 173

Labour Party
  educational policy, 153, 166,
  193
  manifesto, 153
Lancaster speech (Crosland), 193
Lansbury, George, 17
Lee, Jennie, 155
Leeds University, 13, 17, 97
Leicestershire, 125, 127, 188, 191
Local authorities
  associations, 175, 187, 189
  elections (1968 and 1969), 191
  electorate, 27
  finances, 27
  powers and duties, 27

relations with central
government, 26, 29, 31, 100,
124, 127, 128, 160, 170, 171,
175, 187
reorganization (*Herbert Report*,
Maud Report and 1971
White Paper), 25, 45, 162, 169
Local Government Acts,
1958, 55
1963, 27
London County Council, 16
London Government Bill (1963),
87
Lloyd, Geoffrey, 83, 87, 97
Lloyd, Selwyn, 65, 107

MacArthur, Brian, 46, 85
Maclure, Stuart, 46, 134
Macmillan, Harold, 35, 36, 81,
90, 110, 136
MacNamara, Robert, 32, 59
Maud Commission and *Report*,
27, 128
Maude, Angus, 17
Maudling, Reginald
as Chancellor, 65
on educational investment, 21,
118
M Ps
and Ministers, 15, 46
prospects, 15
role, 119–21, 165
Mendès-France, Pierre, 75
Middle schools, 35, 57, 60, 78
Miles, Margaret, 46
Miles-Davies, A., 83
Mill, J. S., 41
Ministers
compared with civil servants, 14,
39–44, 138, 150–51
junior Ministers, 54, 55
length of office, 158, 159
salaries and prospects, 14
two or one, 105–7
see also Parliamentary
Secretary
Mitchell, Robert, 185

Morant, Robert, 150, 180
Morrell, Derek, 29, 73, 150, 180,
187
Morrison, Charles, 119
Morrison, Herbert, 22
Moser, Claus, 47

National Advisory Council for
the Training and Supply of
Teachers (N A C S T T), 89,
131, 132, 173
Eleventh Report, 173
Ninth Report, 175, 176
Report on Demand and Supply,
1960–1980, 68, 81
National Association of
Schoolmasters, 190
National Council for Educational
Technology, 41, 51, 52, 147,
176, 177
N E D C (National Economic
Development Council) Report,
65
National Foundation for
Educational Research
(N F E R), 29, 67
National Plan, 123, 145
National Union of Students, 47,
190, 192
National Union of Teachers, 45,
134, 147, 156, 175, 187, 190,
194, 197
Nationalization, Crosland's
attitudes to, 17, 19, 20
Nenk, David, 29, 73, 124, 150
Newens, Stanley, 119
New Society, 18, 29, 46, 143
Newsom, John
as Chief Education Officer,
Hertfordshire, 29
and Public Schools
Commission, 29, 51, 146
Newsom Report (*Half Our*
Future), 18, 24, 91, 92, 102,
132, 138, 174, 191
Boyle's preface to, 24, 58, 93, 94
New Statesman, 55, 119

Nicolson, Nigel, 72
Nield, Robert, 18, 74
1922 Committee, 119
Nutting, Anthony, 72

Objectives, educational, 16, 28,
    31, 80, 116, 163, 164
Opportunity State and
    educational testing, 23, 90
Opposition, 165
  Conservative, 78
Overseas students' fees, 147, 165,
    166, 178

Parliamentary debates, 166
Parliamentary Labour Party, 166,
    196
  Education Group, 165
Parliamentary Private Secretary,
    165, 185
Parliamentary questions, 156
Parliamentary Secretary
  Boyle's and Crosland's views of
    role, 54, 55, 86–8, 157, 185
  Boyle's appointment and
    activities as, 54–7, 65, 85
  role of junior Ministers, 15, 40,
    153, 157, 165, 174
Part, Antony, 29, 83, 98
Patent Office, 48, 179
Permanent Secretaries, 73, 83,
    101, 111, 123, 131, 150, 157,
    196
Pile, William, 29, 30, 138
Planning, educational, 28
  in DES (Planning Branch),
    31, 51, 59, 147, 176, 177, 183
Plowden Committee, setting up,
    66, 173
Plowden, Lady, 173
Plowden Report, 14, 17, 18, 21,
    23, 53, 130, 132, 135, 147, 174
  survey of parental attitudes,
    18
Plummer, Leslie, 46, 122
Polytechnics, 40, 52, 128, 194, 195
  White Paper on (1966), 147
Populism and progressivism, 17

Positive discrimination
  Boyle's attitude to, 17, 18
  and Plowden Report, 18
Prentice, Reginald, 50, 189
Press, and education, 14, 16, 21,
    109
Pressure groups, 160, 175
Price, Christopher, 119, 165, 185
Primary education, 126, 127
Prime Minister
  appointment of civil servants,
    181
  appointment of Ministers, 35,
    105
  authority over Ministers, 35
  chances of becoming, 70
  DES relations with, 34, 89,
    90, 102, 160
Private Secretaries, 54, 81,
    99–101, 157, 158
Profumo, John, 95
Programme budgeting,
    Crosland's views on, 32, 59, 163
Public Accounts Committee, and
    universities, 196
Public expenditure control, 163
Public Expenditure Survey
  Committee (PESC), 123, 168
Public Investment Programme,
    104
Public schools, Crosland's
    policy on, 20, 52, 155, 196
Public Schools Commission,
    appointment of, 36, 41, 42,
    51, 146, 160, 177, 184, 196, 197

Race relations, and Boyle, 14
Race Relations Act (1968), and
    Boyle, 54
Raison, Timothy, 18, 119, 133
Rate-support grants, 27, 124, 125,
    171
Redhead, Edward, 156
Rée, Harry, 46
Regional policy, 163, 164
Rehn, Gösta, 28
Research, educational, 57, 66, 190
Rippon, Geoffrey, 105, 106

Robbins, Lionel (Lord), 106
Robbins Report, 88, 91, 92, 132, 133
  Boyle's acceptance of, 66
  demand for places, 21, 24, 90
  secretariat, 47
Rossetti, H. F., 98
Routh, Andrew, 57

Salisbury, Lord, 77, 94
School-leaving age, raising of, 21, 26, 53, 57, 67, 84, 90, 104, 130, 138, 139, 198
Schools
  Branch, DES, 84, 198
  buildings and programmes, 19, 26, 30, 103, 125, 160, 170, 177, 197
  establishment of, 26, 125
Schools Council, 130
  decision to create, 40, 67, 172
  and Morrell, 29
  role, 172, 173
Science
  combined with education, 25
  policy for, 25, 152, 158
  Research Council, 198
Scotland, 25, 162
Secondary education
  'for all', 23, 28, 42
  modern schools, 23
  reorganization, 31, 40, 50, 51, 82, 84, 90, 94, 115, 125, 158, 188
  Circular 10/65, 49, 52, 78, 146, 160, 175, 176, 188, 189, 191
  Circular 10/70, 49, 52, 119, 175
Secondary School Examinations Council, 67
Selection in education (eleven-plus), 20, 22, 52, 57, 92, 105, 186
  Boyle's attitude to, 19, 78, 82
  Crosland's attitude to, 20
  G factor and testing, 23, 66, 92
Shadow Cabinet, 105, 110, 114
Sharpe, Evelyn, 79

Shearman, Harold, minority report to Robbins, 107
Short, Edward, 44, 153
Simon, Jack, 140
Simon of Wythenshawe, Lord, 132
Smieton, Mary, 45, 99, 170
Social demand for education, 21, 22, 164
Social Science Research Council, 147
Social sciences policy, 163, 164, 165, 168
Sociology of education, 20, 24, 92, 172, 184, 186
Special educational services, 55, 199
Standing Committees, 87
Stansted decision, 52, 182
Statement of Intent (TUC), 66
Stevens, Roger, 107
Stewart, Michael, 12, 49, 152, 153, 188
Student dissent and relations, 109, 110, 121
Suez crisis, 17, 54, 57, 72, 81
Sunday Times, 17
Supply, Ministry of (Boyle as Parliamentary Secretary), 69
Sweden
  Board of Education, 77
  comprehensive schools, 42, 50, 190
  Ministry of Finance, 71
  objectives and planning, 164
  Prime Ministers, 118
  research on comprehensives, 190
  social democratic government, 16, 77

Tanner, J. M., 47, 133
Tawney, R. H., 21, 49
Taxation policy, 168
Taylor, Lord, Study Group, 67
  Report, 52, 167
Teachers
  associations, 160, 175, 176, 187, 189

Teachers–*contd*
disqualification of, 55
'fourteen points' (Crosland),
    41, 46, 53, 191, 192
NACSTT, 46, 53, 132
pensions, 48, 199
salaries, 26, 124, 171
    Boyle's reconstruction of
    Burnham Committee, 57, 68,
    95
    Burnham Committee, 26
supply, 26, 46, 57, 81, 83, 89, 90,
    95, 104, 152, 158, 172, 192, 193
staffing ratios and size of classes,
    170, 171
Supply Branch, DES, 29, 30,
    170, 177
training, 21, 37, 68, 81, 90, 138,
    170
women, wastage of, 82
Technical colleges, 194, 195 *see
    also* Further education
Technical Education (White
    Paper, 1956), 20, 113
Thatcher, Margaret
    Circular 10/70, 49, 51, 118, 175,
    176
    educational policies, 17
*The Times Educational
    Supplement*, 49, 134, 174
Thorneycroft, Peter, 56, 158
Trade, Board of, 48, 179, 181, 182,
    185, 186, 197, 198
Trade and Industry, Department
    of, 29
    comparison with DES, 34,
    156, 158, 160, 162
Transport House, 166, 167
Treasury
    controls over education, 34, 37,
    81, 82, 86, 93, 94, 102–4,
    111, 124, 160, 167, 177, 186
    roles played, 38, 44, 96, 112, 114
    Boyle's views on, 16, 17, 39, 75,
    76, 112–14, 137
    Crosland's views on, 16, 38, 39,
    168, 179, 198

Boyle as junior Treasury
    Minister, 53, 57, 81, 113
Trend, Burke, 108, 111
Tribune group, 119
Two-tier schools, 190

Under-Secretaries, role and
    status of, 40, 41, 181, 182,
    184, 193
Universities
    DES relations with, 25, 88,
    128, 147, 160, 185, 195, 196
    entry to, 93
    grants to, 88
    technological, 25, 93
University Grants Committee
    (UGC), 25, 93, 107, 128,
    196

Vaizey, John, 21, 45, 46, 91, 92,
    93, 155, 185, 186
Vice-Chancellors, 155, 177
Vosper, D. F. (Lord Runcorn),
    199

Wales, 162
    government of education of, 25
    university of, 177
Watt, David, 123
Weaver, Toby, 24, 73, 83, 98,
    105, 123, 143
Wedgwood Benn, Anthony, 12
Weights and Measures, 48, 179
Welsh CAT, 178
West Riding, 127
Whitelaw, William, 46, 122
Williams, Shirley, 17
Wilson, Harold
    in power, 14
    relations with Crosland, 35, 160
Woodfield, Philip, 99
Woolton, Lord, 183
Woolwich speech (Crosland), 193,
    195
Wright, John, 185

Young, Michael, 46, 133, 185